PRAISE FOR
WADE ROWLAND'S
BOOKS ON BROADCASTING

Canada Lives Here: The Case for Public Broadcasting
(2015), by Wade Rowland

"This is an urgent, important and timely book
about how public broadcasting in Canada is being
eviscerated. The CBC has been abandoned, both
by a government that should support it, but won't,
and by a management culture unable to handle the
political, economic and technological headwinds
affecting all media but especially public broadcasting. The CBC was once Canada's greatest cultural gift to the world; it is now in a perilous state
of programming and financial decrepitude. But
it's not yet lost. Wade Rowland gives us reasons
for optimism, showing us how the CBC might
yet be saved—if it can demonstrate that it can
engage Canadians as citizens first, not just as de-
liverables to commercial and political interests."
—Jeffrey Dvorkin,
Lecturer and Director of the Journalism Program,
University of Toronto (Scarborough)

Saving the CBC: Balancing Profit and Public Service
(2013), by Wade Rowland

"This book should be read by everyone who gives

a damn about Canada and the publicly owned broadcaster that unites us in telling our own stories on radio and television. Wade Rowland convincingly documents the slow, politically directed erosion of the CBC and he has the expertise to show us how to save, and expand, this vital component in Canadian life. Will we listen to him? I hope to God we have enough sense to do so."

—Farley Mowat, OC (1921-2014),
one of Canada's most widely read
and respected authors.

"Consider this an impassioned polemic—'debate' is far too sedate—ignited by the CBC's degradation in recent years and fed by cold rage against the main culprits, yet with a surprising optimism about future possibilities.

—Rick Salutin,
author and *Toronto Star* columnist

"If you're looking for the first principles required for effective public broadcasting in Canada in the twenty-first century, Wade Rowland has articulated them here with clarity and eloquence. No excuses left for failure to act—except for that most Canadian of realities: the lack of political will."

—Kealy Wilkinson,
Broadcast Consultant and Executive Director,
Canadian Broadcast Museum Foundation

Canada
Lives Here

Canada Lives Here

The Case for Public Broadcasting

WADE ROWLAND

.ll.

Cover design: Debbie Geltner
Cover image: Terry Mosher
Prepared for the press by Linda Leith and Katia Grubisic
Author photo: Christine Collie Rowland
Book design: WildElement.ca

Printed and bound in Canada by Imprimerie Gauvin.

Library and Archives Canada Cataloguing in Publication

Rowland, Wade, 1944-, author
Canada lives here : the case for public broadcasting / Wade Rowland.

Includes bibliographical references and index.
Issued in print and electronic formats.

ISBN 978-1-927535-82-0 (paperback).--ISBN 978-1-927535-83-7 (epub).--
ISBN 978-1-927535-84-4 (mobi).--ISBN 978-1-927535-85-1 (pdf)

     1. Public broadcasting--Canada. 2. Canadian Broadcasting
Corporation.
  I. Title.
HE8689.9.C3R65 2015   384.540971   C2015-9034221
                                          C2015-903423-X

The publisher gratefully acknowledges the support of the Canada Council for the Arts.

Linda Leith Publishing Inc.
P.O. Box 322, Victoria Station
Westmount QC H3Z 2V8
Canada

www.lindaleith.com

For my brother
Douglas Charles Rowland,
BA, MA, CD,
Queen's Jubilee Medal,
scholar, naval officer, parliamentarian,
public servant, diplomat,
inveterate *pro bono* volunteer,
and the rock in my life.

On the occasion of his
seventy-fifth birthday
June 2015

CONTENTS

INTRODUCTION

Media scholars like to argue over whether the growing complexity of the world drives innovation in communication, or improved communication leads to growing global complexity. It's a moot point: for most of us the question that matters is, how do I keep up? As Canada prepared itself for a pivotal federal election in the autumn of 2015, issues of a stubbornly stagnant economy, of austerity versus stimulus, of terrorism and security, of transparency and democratic values, of carbon taxes versus cap-and-trade, of pipelines versus railcars, of financing urban infrastructure, of multiculturalism and reasonable accommodation, of the mechanics of coalition governments, of crime prevention, of the cold war comeback, of military engagement in the Middle East, of doctor-assisted suicide … a host of concerns each briefly took their turns at centre stage. These issues shared a common characteristic: they were enormously complicated, they were all important, and they were understood by only a small minority of a dwindling number of voters.

The problem of democracies having to deal with complex issues is not new. Early in the twentieth century, the American journalist Walter Lippmann and philosopher John Dewey butted heads over the conundrum of how a modern democracy might govern itself, given that so few citizens had the time, ability, or inclination to study the issues of the day. For Lippmann, the only non-violent answer lay in governance by an intellectual and technical elite who would rule, in the public interest, on the basis of "manufactured consent," a consensus built around "necessary illusions" created at election times using the tools of modern propaganda.

Dewey was not ready to give up on the people, and advocated an enhanced public sphere, where citizens could learn about the issues from informed journalists, dramatists, artists, and other impartial purveyors of information, and debate among themselves, forming a truly democratic consensus that would determine the outcome of electoral contests.

In the tormented history of the intervening century, both Lippmann's despairing views and Dewey's more optimistic outlook have had their moments of popularity and plausibility. But it is Dewey's confidence in people's ability to engage in critical, reflective thought and dialogue that is central to the ideas expressed in this book. For it is the role of a public broadcaster like the Canadian Broadcasting Corporation to ensure that public space, free of vested interests and their propaganda, is made available so that citizen-democrats can constructively tackle the difficult problems facing their nation. Private, commercial media may play a part in providing that democratic public space, but only a public broadcaster can be expected reliably to serve Dewey's informed and alert citizens, and not the crafters of necessary illusions and the manufacturers of consent.

The year prior to the most recent Canadian federal election was a watershed for CBC/Radio-Canada*: 2014 was the year that saw the public broadcaster lose its iconic, eighty-one-year-old sports franchise, NHL hockey, to a private media conglomerate. It was the year in which a federal government apparently hostile to the very notion of public broadcasting reduced the CBC's already shrunken public subsidy to $28 per Canadian, or fifty-six cents a week, which is about one-third of the *average* provided by the other industrial democracies of the OECD to their public broadcasters; less than eight percent of the amount each Canadian pays annually to fund that other much-revered national institution, Medicare.

This was not the first, or even the biggest, financial crisis the CBC has faced in recent history. Far from it.

---

* The public broadcaster is officially known as the Canadian Broadcasting Corporation/Société Radio-Canada (CBC/SRC) in acknowledgement of its bilingual mandate. In these pages, "CBC" and "the Corporation" refer to the broadcaster as a corporate enterprise. "CBC Television" and "CBC Radio" refer to the English-language networks unless otherwise noted.

In 1990, draconian cuts of $108 million led to the shutting down or downsizing of eleven regional broadcasting centres. In 1995, a further budget cut of $125 million led the then-president Tony Manera to resign in protest rather than be responsible for gutting the institution he had hoped to nurse back to health. Since that time, the government subsidy to the corporation (formally, the Parliamentary Appropriation) had crept slowly back up to 1990 levels, but when indexed to inflation, actual contributions from the federal government in 2015 were down by some seventy percent. This dramatic decline had been, to some extent, compensated for by television advertising income, but with the loss of the hockey franchise, that too dropped off precipitously.

As if the financial straits were not enough, the CBC, like broadcasters everywhere, was facing tumultuous change in the industrial and technological environment, a transformation that called into question the foundational assumptions of the industry as they had been understood for a hundred years. Questions were being raised about the relevance of the concept of public broadcasting in an environment in which the very term "broadcasting" often seemed an anachronism. It was a perfect storm, which threatened to tear apart what had for generations been celebrated as the nation's most important cultural institution.

Through it all, the CBC's legal and regulatory mandate remained unchanged. It must make high-quality, distinctively Canadian programming available from coast to coast to coast in both French and English. It must serve aboriginal audiences in several native languages. It must maintain regional broadcasting centres, and expensive over-the-air networks in radio and television, with all the ancillary equipment and real estate. It still must staff and program two French-language radio networks; two English radio networks; television networks in both languages; cable news networks in both languages; elaborate Websites in both languages; and buy and maintain the necessary equipment and real estate.[1]

While the CBC's financial problems require political solutions, the technical revolution can be counted on to follow its own course, driven by forces beyond the control of any individual state or enterprise. It will be a decade or more before this storm subsides and the survivors settle in to new and sustainable modes of creating and distributing cultural products, either for profit or in the public interest. If there is a silver lining for the CBC, it's that the technological transformation is offering new possibilities for richer and more efficient ways of communicating with its audiences.

The upheaval in broadcasting has been brought on by the digital revolution, the convergence of all media onto a single binary format of ones and zeros. Reduced to bits and bytes, everything from television pictures to text, photographs, and recorded music can be stored on computers for instant retrieval and streamed or downloaded over the Internet to an array of compact, portable viewing and listening devices. In this context of transformation, new possibilities are opening up for any broadcaster with adequate resources and imaginative leadership to reinvigorate itself. Audiences are not shrinking, but fragmenting. Their basic needs and wants remain largely unchanged; it is the opportunities to serve those needs and satisfy those interests that are exploding. Thus, the responsibility of public-service broadcasters like the CBC will also remain much the same: to ensure that the public is well-served with high-quality information, education, and entertainment aimed at advancing civic and societal, rather than commercial, ends.

In practice, this amounts mainly to repairing market failures endemic to the private broadcasting industry: the failure to produce high-quality, objective news and information programming in sufficient volume; the failure to produce authentically Canadian dramatic programming; the failure to put viewers' interests ahead of the interests of advertisers; the failure to adequately serve minority preferences and concerns; the failure to actively foster social cohesion and understanding—the general failure of privately owned, commercial media to serve their audiences as citizens first and consumers second. The failures will remain the same, because they stem from a common cause: the overriding necessity for commercial enterprises to make a profit. But they will exhibit themselves in different ways on new and emerging platforms for distribution.

"Adequate resources" and "imaginative leadership" are the two key concepts here for the CBC. While the CBC struggles to survive with its $28 per capita subsidy, in the European Union, where programs produced by national public broadcasters regularly dominate top-ten popularity charts, public funding ranges from $180 per capita in Norway to $124 in Germany to $97 in the UK, all the way down to last-place Italy at $38 per citizen per year.

As for the quality of leadership at CBC, it might be said to speak for itself. For example, when the Canadian Radio-television and Telecommunications Commission (CRTC) announced its plans to reduce regulatory demands for Canadian content (Can-con) production in 2015, senior CBC management greeted the news as an opportunity for the corporation to "significantly increase foreign content"—and associated revenue—on its specialty channels *documentary* and *ICI ARTV*.[2] Earlier administrations had placed CBC English television on an unabashedly commercial, ratings-driven footing. Still earlier, managers had shut down regional broadcasting centres, which are at the core of the CBC mandate, in order to save money. These are not the responses one might hope for from a public broadcaster.

But it has to be conceded that for decade after decade, federal governments have refused to provide the predictable, long-term funding necessary to coherent management of an organization as large and complex as the public broadcaster. Senior managers, most with little or no broadcast industry experience, have been forced to cope with what amounts to a perpetual financial crisis, in the ways they know best—through crude balance-sheet surgery. Resistance to government funding cuts from presidents, Boards of Directors, and Board chairs has been, with some rare exceptions, deferential and ineffective—or non-existent. In the wake of the 2014 budget cuts, nine former CBC directors, including a former CBC president, were concerned enough about this passivity to write to the chair of the Board of Directors, suggesting that he and other directors had forgotten that they "are trustees of a statutory mandate based on the maintenance of a capacity within the Corporation to broadcast, inform and certainly to create," and calling on board members "to clearly and publicly inform the Government that these cuts will effectively eviscerate CBC/Radio-Canada and will ultimately bring about the demise of this important and valued national public service." Calls for the resignation of President Hubert Lacroix came from inside and outside the CBC, on grounds that he had moral and statutory obligations not to cooperate in the demolition of the public institution he had been hired to manage.

Through much of 2014, the country's media and telecommunications regulator, the CRTC, was holding hearings into the need for new rules to better match the evolving technical realities of the media it governed. Hundreds of individual Canadians, unions, industry associations, interest groups, and businesses took part in the sessions, cheerily dubbed "Let's Talk Television." One result was a series of new directives from the regulator designed to rationalize the public funding system for supporting the production of Canadian content, to prioritize quality over quantity. This was deemed necessary because private broadcasters and producers had been using hundreds of millions of dollars a year in Canadian content subsidies to build a thriving industry that specialized in programs that fit technical, bureaucratic definitions of Can-con, but were actually designed to be sold abroad, in order to maximize return on investment. Relatively little had been produced in terms of authentically, unmistakably, Canadian programming in any genre. And yet that was where the market failure was most obvious and damaging. It was an activist regulator that reported on its public hearings in 2015, revising Can-con regulations, ordering cable companies to change their marketing and pricing strategies, especially the practice of selling groups of channels in prepackaged bundles, to make them more consumer-friendly, and more likely to limit the problem of free-riding bundled channels of dubious merit. Pick-and-pay would be the new catchword, meaning that consumers would have new freedom to select only the individual channels they wanted.

And when the president of Bell Media was revealed in the press to have directly interfered with CTV News coverage of the CRTC announcements in March 2015, CRTC commissioner Jean-Pierre Blais reacted immediately with a public statement worth quoting at some length. Noting pointedly that that the Broadcasting Act entrusted the CRTC with defending freedom of expression and journalistic independence, he continued:

That a regulated company does not like one of the CRTC's rulings is one thing. The allegation, however, that the largest communication company in Canada is manipulating news coverage is disturbing. Holding a radio or television licence is a privilege that comes with important obligations that are in the public interest, especially in regards to high-quality news coverage and reporting. An informed citizenry cannot be sacrificed for a company's commercial interests. Canadians can only wonder how many times corporate interests may have been placed ahead of the fair and balanced news reporting they expect from their broadcasting system.

It was a source of disappointment for many that in its announcements at the conclusion of the "Let's Talk Television" hearings, the CRTC made no mention of the CBC or the role of public broadcasting in the evolving media ecosystem. If ever there was a case to be made for the necessity of an independent, well-funded public-service broadcaster, Bell Media had made it. More than that, unsolicited submissions to the hearings from the general public had overwhelmingly called on the regulator to protect the health and integrity of public broadcasting in whatever regulatory reform might be forthcoming. Dark suspicions were aroused that the Conservative government of Prime Minister Stephen Harper had made plans to "deal with" the CBC following the 2015 election, and that the CRTC had been instructed to avoid the subject for that reason; rumours to that effect were abundant, but could not be confirmed.

Also in 2014, provoked by the NHL hockey deal, the Senate Transportation and Communication Committee launched hearings into the role of the CBC, which ran concurrently with the CRTC hearings. The committee, headed by Liberal Senator Dennis Dawson, was dominated by Conservatives, most of them ideologically antipathetic to the public broadcaster. But Dawson promised a credible result: "(Conservatives) know if this institution [the Senate] is to survive, it has to be credible ... They know that it will not be credible if we go out there and have a report that is perceived as being an extension of the PMO or the Conservative caucus."[3]

The polling organization Angus Reid Institute saw in all of this activity an opportunity for a major survey of Canadian attitudes to culture, the CBC and the CRTC.[4] It reported early in 2015 that attitudes toward the CRTC in all regions of the country were "generally favourable." And, when asked if "Canada still needs specific protection policies and support from government for Canadian culture to survive," seventy percent of respondents answered yes; nearly fifty percent felt that Canadian culture "would be completely swallowed up by American and foreign culture" without those safeguards. The poll found that eighty percent of Canadians hold an "overall favourable view" of the CBC; the more engaged with CBC the respondents were, the higher their opinion of the broadcaster. It also found that most respondents, while (often wildly) overestimating the per-capita size of the CBC's government subsidy, at the same time felt that the amount was either "about right" or too low.

Regional differences in attitudes to the CBC were relatively small, ranging from eighty-eight percent "favourable" or "very favourable" in Quebec, and eighty-seven percent in Atlantic Canada, to a low of about seventy percent in Alberta and Saskatchewan. Alberta and Saskatchewan shared the highest "unfavourable" rankings, but they were only twenty-eight and twenty-seven percent, respectively. "Very favourable" responses were highest from the better educated and from women. Broken down according to political affiliation, attitudes to the CBC were generally favourable among seventy-six percent of Conservatives, ninety-one percent of Liberals, eighty-four percent of NDP supporters and ninety-four percent of Green Party voters.

These were not the kinds of figures likely to warm the hearts of CBC abolitionists; indeed, the broadcaster's supporters could legitimately find solace in the Angus Reid numbers. The poll confirmed other data showing that the CBC audience skewed toward older Canadians, its most devoted listeners and viewers likely to be fifty-five or older—a growing demographic. Nevertheless, fully a third of respondents under thirty-five also regarded themselves as committed users of CBC radio and television services.

Perhaps not surprisingly, those who tuned in to CBC radio and television programming most often held the services in high esteem, ninety-nine percent of frequent listeners and viewers reporting favourable or very favourable impressions.

In the summer of 2014, the CBC announced what it called a strategy for sustainability, dubbed, with unconscious irony, "A space for us all." A cornerstone was massive layoffs (fifteen hundred employees across the system over five years, in addition to 657 job cuts announced earlier that year). But there was also to be a fundamental shift in the corporation's priorities, away from conventional radio and television toward online and wireless delivery of digital content. Cheaper programming, delivered more cheaply. Very little of that content would be produced by the CBC; rather, it would be commissioned or purchased from private producers. The exceptions would be news, current affairs, and radio, the announcement said. But those areas had already been dramatically downsized in previous austerity moves, and the corporation admitted its plan involved cutting back local evening television newscasts from ninety to sixty or thirty minutes. It also involved further cuts to in-house documentary production, most of which the CBC would be outsourcing to private producers. New "content" aimed at mobile devices such as tablets, laptops, and smartphones was promised, but few specifics were offered. The corporation did commit itself to producing, over the succeeding five years, more "cutting edge" comedy series and at least three television dramas of "cable quality" for English-language television, which presumably meant matching the production values of HBO or AMC blockbusters such as *Breaking Bad* or *True Detective*. It hoped to finance these ambitions plans through co-production deals with other Canadian and American broadcasters, which immediately raised questions about whether such productions would represent Canadian, or merely commercial, values. If the latter, why bother?

The viability of the plan was called into question on other counts when the CBC publicly broached the money-saving idea of shutting down some of its over-the-air transmitters and moving content onto online delivery platforms. The CRTC flatly refused permission, not just to the CBC but to private broadcasters as well, arguing that OTA broadcasting would remain an essential service for the foreseeable future.

While there may be sound logic in the public broadcaster's expansion of its digital, online services, the experience among other broadcasters is that this is not a money-saving strategy, since personnel costs must remain high if standards are to be maintained. Some money may well be saved if conventional television and radio services, and their costs, are curtailed, but there is no evidence that audiences are prepared to switch their consumption habits any time soon. In other words, if the CBC is to maintain its audience, it will have to serve both conventional and digital platforms. Certainly, more and more Canadians are using portable digital devices to access content of all kinds, but it is also true that conventional television viewing across Canada had actually showed a slight increase over the fifteen years beginning in 1993, from twenty-five to twenty-eight hours a week.[5] This has been attributed to a sharp improvement in the quality of programming, which has come with the rising popularity of subscription television, and to advances in viewing technology that make home theatre arrangements affordable. (By contrast, Canadians were viewing, on average, only about five hours a week of Internet-delivered television, although those numbers are trending upward.)

If it is possible at this stage in the media environment's rapid evolution to see a trend, it may be that audiences everywhere are looking to conventional television for richer cinematic experiences represented by American cable or BBC-style miniseries, and to their portable devices for news and light entertainment of the kind traditionally delivered by network television and radio, and by YouTube and its clones. If this is the case, the CBC survival strategy could well be on the right track, at least in principle. But quite obviously the corporation does not have the revenue necessary to satisfy either half of the equation. The BBC, which is pursuing a similar strategy and succeeding on both digital and conventional fronts, receives funding from licence fees of about $6 billion a year, six times the CBC's government subsidy. The BBC's budget more accurately reflects what it costs to run a successful, sustainable public-service broadcaster in a modern democracy.

CHAPTER 1

A UNIQUE HISTORY

Canadians spend more time watching television, listening to the radio, and using the Internet than they do at their paid jobs, and in fact more time than they devote to any activity other than sleeping—about sixty-two hours a week, on average. That fact alone makes it obvious that the nature and quality of what we're seeing and hearing makes a difference in our lives, helping to shape who we are, as individuals and as a society. For most of us, these media are our most important sources of information about the world that lies beyond our immediate experience. It's important that broadcasters provide this service accurately and responsibly.

Radio, the granddaddy of today's ubiquitous wireless media, amazed the world with its introduction in the last years of the nineteenth century. It was initially employed as a wireless adaptation of the telegraph, and then as a new kind of telephone, a device for point-to-point communication. But in the years immediately following World War I, the new technology's potential as a medium of mass communication—of broadcasting—was beginning to be understood and explored in Europe, the UK and North America. Broadcasting's pioneers could see that radio's ability to reach scattered populations simultaneously with messages of entertainment and information was a game-changer. It didn't matter where listeners lived: radio could reach right into their homes, and it arrived free of charge.

The response to the opportunities presented by this technological wonder would quickly resolve itself into two essentially different attitudes. Business entrepreneurs saw the potential for enormous profit in what broadcast radio could offer to advertisers: audiences, from coast to coast, from every walk of life, far more extensive than anything provided by mass-circulation newspapers or magazines, until then the main vehicles for advertising national brands. On the other hand, some politicians, social activists, and educators saw in radio fabulous potential for enormously expanding the public space in which democracy's consensus-forging conversations could take place— a medium of mass education, quality information and entertainment, and for the cultivation of cultural literacy.

Whether these disparate goals were mutually exclusive was a matter of controversy from the beginning, and the continuing debate will be touched on frequently is succeeding chapters of this book. For the moment, it's important to know that in most of Europe, in the UK, in Australia, and to an extent in Canada, it was the second, public-service, opportunity that was embraced politically and in the public mind as radio developed, and later, as television was introduced. In most places, commercial applications of the new media were initially either banned or severely restricted. The exception was the United States, where the decision was made to turn the medium over to the business entrepreneurs, in the belief that free market forces would ensure the listening public was well served.

In both instances, radio would eventually emerge as a tightly regulated industry, in contrast, for example, to newspapers and other print media. In most countries, state-supported public enterprises were given a monopoly on broadcasting, along with a strong public-service mandate to fulfill, but even in the US, broadcasters were expected to provide public payback for their access to the airwaves.[6]

In the United Kingdom all radio broadcasting was taken over in 1922 by a government-backed consortium of radio manufacturers named the British Broadcasting Company. It was licensed by the Royal Mail, which was already responsible for telegraphy and the telephone system. Advertising on the airwaves was banned, and the company's operations were funded by a license fee on radio receivers. In 1926 the company was replaced by a commission representing the public rather than manufacturers, and the enterprise was renamed the British Broadcasting Corporation (BBC). To emphasize its independence from Parliament, and the fact that it was a public service and not just an ordinary business, the BBC was organized under a Royal Charter rather than routine corporate legislation.

In America, after an initial chaotic period in which the courts required the Department of Commerce to issue a licence to any American citizen who asked for one, the Federal Radio Commission in 1927 began the rationing of licences and allocation of frequencies to private broadcasters, on the condition that they use the privilege as "the public interest, convenience and necessity" required. The Commission had no further control over programming, except to ensure that candidates for public office were allocated equal air time. This meant, in effect, that radio was to be treated as a minimally regulated, privately owned utility. The question of how to finance the industry was resolved in favour of commercial sponsorship of programming, a plan that won out over such alternatives as endowments, foundations, and federal subsidies only after many months of intense debate. Secretary of Commerce Herbert Hoover, for one, stated flatly, "The ether is a public medium and must be used for the public good. It is quite inconceivable that it should be used for advertising."[7]

Early Canadian radio broadcasting developed along lines similar to the American experiment, although on a much smaller scale.[8] But while most stations were privately owned and advertising-supported, public broadcasting got an early boost when, in 1924, the government-owned Canadian National Railway (CNR) began building a coast-to-coast network of radio stations to provide information and entertainment to railway passengers in special parlour cars equipped with receivers and headphones. The broadcasting stations dotting the transcontinental rail line could of course be heard by anyone in the surrounding territory. The initial aims of the network were to increase ticket sales and solidify corporate morale. The railway had been patched together from several bankrupt private lines in the post-war recession, and the radio service was intended by CNR president Henry Thornton to create a family atmosphere among the thousands of employees scattered across the continent. But Thornton also had a more ambitious vision, of the kind of public-interest broadcasting that was emerging all over Europe, but which Parliament had so far failed to implement.

In the nine years of its operation, the CNR radio network established many firsts. In 1927, it marked the diamond jubilee of Confederation with special programming that united the country with simultaneous broadcasts over a national network of stations connected by 5,500 km of telephone and telegraph lines. In 1929 the network began three hours a week of scheduled national programming. Its offerings included complete comic operas, school broadcasts, Saturday afternoon concerts from the Toronto Symphony Orchestra, and a series of high-concept dramas, based on significant events in Canadian history and directed by the distinguished British stage director Tyrone Guthrie.

RATIONALE FOR REGULATION

The impulse of governments everywhere to impose controls on radio broadcasting may seem odd, given the long-standing tradition of press freedom enjoyed by thriving book, newspaper and magazine industries of the time. If these earlier mass media were protected from government intervention by the strong cultural biases toward freedom of expression in democratic societies, why was radio different? The explanation lies in the way the technology works.

Both radio and television transmit information in the form of radiation within certain portions (wavelengths) of the electromagnetic spectrum. Since the discovery of electromagnetic fields and their properties in the nineteenth century, those wavelengths capable of being used for practical, wireless communication have been thought of as a public resource, like a great river, or the atmosphere. In the absence of any clear understanding of how radio waves propagate, early experimenters used the analogy of ripples that spread in a pond whose surface is disturbed by a stone. The medium through which radio waves travelled (at the speed of light) had yet to be discovered—the phenomenon is still not completely understood—and so radio signals were described as travelling through the air or "ether," propagated by "airwaves." While a telegraph or telephone line carrying electrical signals might be personal or corporate property, the "air" belonged to no one and to everyone, and to prevent its being monopolized or polluted by private interests, it had to be regulated by government.

Because only a limited slice of the electromagnetic field is suitable for radio transmission over long distances, the problem of spectrum allocation arose early in the history of radio. If transmitters were to avoid interfering with one another's signals (as they often did), they had to operate on different radio frequencies or wavelengths, and the allocation of those frequencies had to be organized both through national regulation and international conventions. Given the public nature of the airwaves, users were assigned the conditional rights of a lessee to their licensed wavelength. Thus, a radio station would be granted a licence to operate on a certain wavelength, on the understanding that it was being given privileged access to a public resource. And, from the earliest days of radio, it was understood that broadcasters owed the public some form of recompense in return for this privilege. As holder of the leases, the public, through their governments, had the right to impose "conditions of use" on the lessees, just as in a rental contract. These included licensing fees, and also, significantly, conditions pertaining to the type and quality of programming being broadcast.

From the beginning, these conditions were framed, in democratic nations, in terms of service to the public, as opposed to service to the state. Even where BBC-style state-sanctioned monopolies held sway (as they did throughout Europe), there was understood to be an important distinction between *public* broadcaster and *state* broadcaster: public broadcasters' funding was supplied at arm's-length from government, usually by some sort of dedicated tax or fee. Public broadcasting needed to be independent, and regulation was designed to ensure it didn't become a tool of either vested private interests or state propagandists. Governments, understanding the value of the public space provided by broadcast media, sought to prevent damage to, or corruption of, that domain.

REGULATION TODAY

The condition of spectrum allocation as it was experienced in radio's early days became less and less central to regulatory policy as technological change, beginning in the mid-1960s, transformed the media landscape with one major disruption after another. First cable and satellite distribution of signals, and then digital convergence and new compression algorithms, and, most recently, delivery via the Internet have made the original circumstance of frequency scarcity less relevant. Where there were once a handful of over-the-air television channels and perhaps a few dozen radio signals available to most households, the figures for both are now in the hundreds.[9] Most of them never see the traditional broadcast spectrum, but are transmitted via coaxial or fibre optic cables and as encrypted, ultra-high-frequency microwave satellite and cellphone signals. This of course raises the question of the continued legitimacy of government regulation of these program delivery services, which we continue—perhaps misleadingly—to call "broadcasting."

Nevertheless, regulation that continues to shape the public-service commitments of broadcasters, both private and public, has ample justification within the more abstract realm of social policy; that is, in the nature of communication itself, recognizing its importance to democracy, social solidarity, and civility. Communication is more than messaging for purposes of getting things done: it involves mutual contact, an exchange. It is the process through which culture is created, sustained and transformed. Dialogue fits this definition, but so do some kinds of broadcasting, in the one-to-many sense. When it works, this latter kind of mass communication moves the listener or viewer to a constructive response, perhaps in the sense of broadened horizons, or deepened affection or empathy, or a determination to act in some way; to improve, to inquire further. In other words, broadcasting, as a cultural enterprise, is a special kind of industry, in that its products affect not only what we do, but what we think. It supplies much of the information and evidence upon which we construct our view of the world and our place in it; our version of common sense. It seems reasonable to conclude that it needs special handling, if only to ensure a balance between civic and commercial interests.

Think of advertising as the discourse of corporate, commercial interests, and then think of the ubiquity of advertising in our lives (the average Canadian is exposed to 25,000 commercials each year on television alone): one begins to have some sense of this kind of corporate communication's power and influence over culture and what we take to be common sense. Almost all of this communication is of the instrumental kind, not really communication at all, but one-way messaging, distributing information (and misinformation), tugging at emotions for commercial ends, issuing commands and calls to action. Much of the content produced by corporate media, when it is not straightforward commercial propaganda (for example, the programs that separate the ads on television) is crafted in ways that support the consumer lifestyle and its values. It's not hard to see how the public-service ethic can get lost in such a prolix information environment, and why there is a perceived need to ensure its preservation through intervention in the market.

Today's digital media, and in particular blogs, and social media like Facebook, Twitter, Instagram, Google+ and a host of other communication applications, have given us all new means of widening our personal spheres of influence, and of shaping the conversation surrounding important social and political issues. But at the same time the very fact that these vehicles are disaggregated, fragmented, and highly personal allows established for-profit mass media enterprises—Big Media and the corporate advertisers that sustain them—to retain by far the loudest and most persistent voices in society. The mass audiences of television's heyday may be slipping away, defecting to the Internet, but the essence of the phenomenon is retained through Web technologies that monitor search patterns, tracking users' interests and preferences. These aggregated, virtual audiences are sold in various demographic breakdowns to advertisers, who can now make personal contact with potential customers via "contextual" ads that appear as if by magic alongside most Internet content, including email. The "audience" is not an obsolete concept; it has been organized and structured for increased commercial efficiency. Big business has said goodbye to mass audiences, and hello to Big Data.

FIXING MARKET FAILURES

Public broadcasters, islands of public-service commitment in the sea of commercial, for-profit media, survive for the simple reason that they're needed. They are, at their best, preserves of reasoned debate as opposed to bombast and propaganda, sanctuaries free of vested interests, state or commercial. They provide entertainment intended to nourish and enrich, rather than merely amuse and generate profit. The public university provides an apt analogy: it exposes students to new ideas and possibilities with a view to enlarging their worlds, but does not dictate choices. As a society, we have agreed that these institutions ought to be publicly funded but essentially self-governing, serving the citizenry rather than the state.

Like universities, public broadcasters enhance lives, both public and private. In formal economic terms, they correct for market failures, which are formally defined by the inability of unregulated markets to produce necessary public goods or services in adequate measure. In broadcasting, market failures may relate to:

- the under-production of domestic programming representing the authentic values, interests, and preoccupations of the nation;
- the under-provision of information, particularly in the form of investigative reporting, documentaries, in-depth news and current affairs;
- the under-production of challenging, "horizon-stretching" programs in all genres;
- the under-production of programs designed to satisfy niche or minority interests of all kinds, particularly those that do not involve consumption of products or services provided by advertisers (i.e. the arts and intellectual content, children's programs);
- the overproduction of content with "negative externalities" (unwanted social impacts) that flow from, for example, gratuitous violence, racism or sexism, or programs presenting false and misleading information as news commentary;
- the overproduction of "reality" programs that exploit the foibles and vulnerabilities of real people as a cheap substitute for scripted drama;
- a generally low level of innovation inherent in commercially sponsored media, which tend to be risk-averse when it comes to challenging audiences with new kinds of programs and presentation.

The interesting economic reason for the under-production of high-value public goods in commercial broadcasting is the fact that any new program on television or radio falls into the subcategory of an "experiential good." These are goods that may have a high perceived value once consumed (the are greatly enjoyed, and provide a benefit), but prior to that may seem undesirable for any number of reasons: a friend may have offered a bad review; the subject matter may seem boring, or too difficult; the advance marketing may be off-putting; the subject matter may be foreign; and so on. For the modern media consumer faced with a plethora of choices, the sensible way to invest scarce recreation time is to watch or listen to something that is a known quantity, sure to be enjoyable. As economists assure us, to take a risk on the unknown when the known is readily at hand is to behave irrationally: the rational economic agent believes that a bird in the hand is better than two in the bush. Thus, in a market that responds to consumer demand, as the commercial media markets do, the familiar gets overproduced, and the new and challenging is under-produced.

In the early days of radio in Canada, the market failure in broadcasting was both obvious and enormous. Cross-border signals permeated the airwaves with programming that was extremely popular—and thoroughly American. In 1928 there were forty US radio stations operating at a power of between 5,000 and 25,000 watts output; in Canada only two stations were broadcasting at 5,000 watts, and most of the others ranged between 10 and 1,000 watts output. The total wattage of American transmitters in 1932 was 680,000 watts; Canadian stations were producing a combined output of 50,000 watts. Canadian content was difficult to find north of the border, and most of what there was could not compete with expensively produced programs coming from New York or Hollywood. The country's population of just ten million in those days was too small and thinly spread to make advertising-supported radio feasible anywhere outside Toronto, Montreal and one or two other urban centres.[10] *Maclean's* magazine lamented the situation in October 1924: "Nine-tenths of the radio fans in this Dominion hear three or four times as many United States stations as Canadian. Few fans, no matter in what part of Canada they live, can regularly pick up more than three or four different Canadian stations; any fan with a good set can 'log' a score of American stations." When the *Toronto Telegram* in 1925 asked its readers to identify their favourite radio stations, the first seventeen positions were occupied by American broadcasters.[11]

Responding to what it saw as an urgent problem of cultural sovereignty, the Liberal government of Prime Minister Mackenzie King in 1928 established a Royal Commission chaired by Sir John Aird. It was to advise Parliament on "the future control, organization and financing of broadcasting." Already, NBC and CBS had affiliate stations in Toronto and Montreal, and the American networks told the inquiry they looked on Canada as a natural northern extension of their markets. The commissioners also visited the UK and Europe, where they were impressed by the public-service monopolies they saw there. The Aird report was released in 1929, on the cusp of the Great Depression, and high on its list of findings was that Canadians wanted to hear Canadian programming. Listeners from coast to coast also felt that there was far too much advertising on Canadian radio stations, a circumstance the commissioners put down to the sparse, dispersed audiences, and the need to generate revenue in what was for most broadcasters a marginal business.

The commission concluded that the nation needed to beef up its broadcasting capabilities from coast to coast to counter the American onslaught, and it recommended the creation of a BBC-style public broadcasting monopoly in Canada. The new broadcaster would take the form of "a government owned and financed company," and would be "vested with the full powers and authority of any private enterprise, it status and duties corresponding to those of a public utility." It was to be financed primarily by license fees on radio equipment, but provision would be made for advertising revenue from the sale of air time for sponsored programs, as a temporary concession to the straitened financial conditions of the Depression era.

Given the makeup of the commission (Aird himself was a banker and a Conservative), it seems clear that the notion of a public broadcasting monopoly did not arise out of any ideological bias.[12] The commissioners had, rather, concluded that the Canadian market, unlike the American, was simply not big enough to support an advertising-based broadcasting sector that would be capable of exploiting the medium's potential, which, it was clear to them, reached far beyond mere entertainment. The report spoke of "education in the broad sense," "public service," "promoting national unity," "fostering a national spirit and interpreting national citizenship," informing the public on "questions of national interest," and shaping the "minds of young people to ideals and opinions that are ... Canadian."[13]

TOWARD A NEW BROADCASTING ACT

Predictably, the Aird Commission's report was hotly contested by Canada's growing commercial broadcasting sector, and more than two years of bitter debate ensued, with leading roles played by the Canadian Association of Broadcasters (CAB), the advertising industry's leading lobby groups, the Canadian Manufacturers' Association, and the nation's newspapers, many of which feared advertising competition from radio.[14] While private station owners and the newspapers had obvious, selfish motives for their objections to the Commission's recommendations, the advertisers' and manufacturers' associations had slightly different concerns. They were worried that a public broadcaster would limit or eliminate advertising on the radio, as the BBC and other European broadcasters had done; the manufacturers were concerned that this would put them at a disadvantage vis-à-vis their US competitors, who were of course free to advertise on American stations that were heard on both sides of the international border.[15]

There was a current of opinion among some private station owners that favoured setting up two parallel broadcasting systems, one public and the other private, as a compromise. But it failed to achieve much traction, since it would not have solved the problem of insufficient advertising revenue to keep stations afloat; in fact, most versions of this plan called for government subsidies to the private sector as well as to the public broadcaster.

Leading the other side of the debate was a citizens' coalition called the Canadian Radio League, organized by two young activists, Graham Spry and Alan Plaunt.[16] The two Oxford graduates were familiar with the nascent BBC in Britain, and they assembled a powerful coalition of interest groups representing education, agriculture, women's issues, religious denominations, labour, and public-service organizations of all kinds, in support of the Aird report and the idea of government-supported public-service broadcasting. Among the League's prominent backers was former Conservative Prime Minister Arthur Meighen, who wrote:

> If left to private enterprise like the magazine and the moving picture, [radio] is bound to cater to the patronage that will reflect in dividends to the stockholders. That is sound commercially, but it will never achieve the best educational ends. ... The amount of fodder that is the antithesis of intellectual that comes over our radios is appalling while

the selection of material for broadcasting remains in commercial hands.[17]

Taking a more positive tack, Spry himself wrote that if Aird's proposals were adopted,

> Canada would have a wonderful instrument of nation-building and a medium through which whatever she has of unique value might be interpreted to the rest of the world. ... For a nation so widespread in its range and so varied in its racial origin, radio broadcasting, intelligently directed, may give us what provincial school systems, local newspapers, and the political system have yet to give us, a single, glowing spirit of nationality making its contribution to the world. ... Here is a great and happy opportunity for expressing, for achieving that which is Canada. It is here now; it may never come again.[18]

The arguments of the Radio League eventually won the debate, though the economic conditions of the time did not allow for a complete victory for the public broadcasting side: the expenditure needed to piece together an entire network of publicly owned stations was a political impossibility given the bleak economic conditions. And so a compromise was adopted when the Conservative government of R.B. Bennett brought in the 1932 Canadian Radio Broadcasting Act. There would a national public broadcaster, called the Canadian Radio Broadcasting Commission (CRBC), that would both create programming and regulate the entire industry. It would be financed by license fees on radio receivers (a funding source that would remain in place until 1958), and a limited amount of indirect, institutional commercial sponsorship. The nation's private stations were put on notice that they were eventually to be absorbed into the public system, when economic conditions permitted. But in the meantime, they were to be allowed to continue operating under private ownership, to fill the yawning gaps in the public network, supplying local programming, and serving local advertisers. Stations were offered the opportunity to become affiliates of the CRBC, accepting contractual commitments to air CRBC-supplied national programming a prescribed number of hours a week. Many signed up with enthusiasm, because the arrangement amounted to a heavy government subsidy for their operations, and they also shared in the advertising revenue associated with many CRBC programs.

Although CRBC programming was well-received by Canadian audiences, the Commission itself proved susceptible to political influence from government ministers, and was criticized for being too cozy with the commercial broadcasters' lobby, the CAB. There were also continuing complaints from the public about the amount of advertising listeners had to endure. On being returned to power in 1936, Mackenzie King, who had been in close contact with the Radio League and its energetic lobbyists, amended the Broadcasting Act, creating the Canadian Broadcasting Corporation (CBC). Like the CRBC, it was to be responsible for supplying network programming, and also for regulating the private sector broadcasters. Its governance structure gave the CBC added protection from government influence, but the power to issue licences was left in the hands of the Department of Transport, which meant that while the CBC could make regulations governing the conduct of private stations, it had no effective way of enforcing them.

PROMOTING NATIONAL UNITY

Conceived as a bulwark against the cross-border blare of American radio programming, the CRBC and its successor, the CBC, were intended to be the cultural equivalent of the great transcontinental railways, the CPR and the CNR, which had successfully drawn the nation's commerce into an east-west alignment against the pull of north-south gravity. The 1932 Broadcasting Act prohibited the foreign ownership or network affiliation of Canadian radio stations. And the CBC was later to be assigned the additional statutory responsibility of promoting unity between anglophone and francophone Canada.

The Act of 1932 had foreseen a single transnational broadcaster that was to be fully bilingual right across the network, broadcasting both French- and English-language programming in its daily schedule. Objections from English-speaking audiences, primarily in Ontario and the West, made this unworkable, and since 1941, there have effectively been two nationwide public broadcasters in the country, the English-language CBC, and the francophone Société Radio-Canada or SRC. Although they are presided over by the same senior management and Board of Directors, there has been surprisingly little cultural exchange between the two networks over the years. However, what cross-fertilization there has been on CBC/Radio-Canada is virtually all there is in Canadian media, in a country still remarkable for its two linguistic solitudes. Private broadcasters have shown no interest in such worthy but unprofitable challenges.

Suspicions would arise periodically that the French-language service was flouting its unity mandate and promoting Quebec nationalism, and following the separatist Parti québécois electoral victory in the province in 1976, Prime Minister Pierre Trudeau ordered the broadcast regulator, the Canadian Radio-Television, Telecommunications Commission (CRTC), to investigate. Another, similar, investigation was ordered by Prime Minister Jean Chrétien in 1995 following the whisker-thin victory for "No" forces in the Quebec referendum on sovereignty. In neither case was any evidence found that SRC had been engaged in propagandizing, or that its news coverage had been biased. What *was* noted was that SRC programming seldom reflected English-Canadian preoccupations, and the coverage of Quebec on the English network, though more complete, was less than adequate.[19] The CBC's statutory obligation to promote national unity had been exposed as a clear constraint on freedom of expression on both sides of the language barrier, and hopelessly incompatible with its responsibility to cover the news fairly and without political bias; it was removed in 1991. The revised mandate requires only that the CBC/SRC, in both languages, "contribute to shared national consciousness and identity."

Despite its nation-building mandate, from its Depression-era beginnings, the CBC network offered, in addition to its own programming, an array of the most popular American radio productions. This was a dual-purpose strategy intended to wean listeners off US stations, while at the same time harvesting the substantial advertising revenue these programs supplied. NBC and CBS hits like *Lux Radio Theater*, *Edgar Bergen and Charlie McCarthy*, *Amos 'n' Andy*, *Fibber McGee and Molly*, *Our Miss Brooks*, *Ma Perkins*, *The Guiding Light* and many more were popular with Canadian audiences who had been listening to them each night on distant American stations.

The strategy initially increased the presence of American programming on Canada's airwaves, but it also helped to assemble a loyal listenership for Canadian programs like the national news read by Charles Jennings, *The Happy Gang, Brave Voyage, John and Judy*, and the perennial *Hockey Night in Canada*, plus the many Canadian performing-arts programs broadcast each week on the CBC network. The popularity of these domestic programs in turn fostered the development of a growing stable of Canadian performers, writers, directors, composers, and musicians, while American content on the network was steadily reduced throughout the middle years of the twentieth century. For some, those were the golden years of Canadian public radio.

CHAPTER 2

TELEVISION AND THE PRIVATE SECTOR'S CONQUEST

The Aird Commission's noble vision of a single, (mostly) advertising-free, public-service-focused broadcasting service for Canada, unattainable for both political and economic reasons, was by the midpoint of the twentieth century effectively dead. Thanks in large measure to the early support of both the CRBC and the CBC, private broadcasting had, by the 1940s, become a highly profitable business, and the idea that private stations should be absorbed into a single, public-service system became politically toxic. As well, the CBC was never given the federal financing necessary to build its own facilities across the nation's vast and often sparsely populated territory. Private radio stations operating in small and remote communities provided invaluable services that the CBC itself could not afford to replace, and so the hybrid, public/private system remained in place for the arrival of television.

In 1952 the CBC opened television stations in Toronto and Montreal, on a three-hour broadcast schedule. The following year, CBC TV carried the coronation of Queen Elizabeth II on a national network, using a relay of RAF and RCAF military jets to speed the film across the Atlantic to Goose Bay, Labrador, and on to Montreal, where it was delivered to the CBC/SRC studios by helicopter. From there it was fed instantaneously to stations across Canada on a newly completed microwave telecom system—the world's longest—and south to ABC and NBC. Just two years later, in 1955, television would be in half of all Canadian households, and there would be nine CBC stations producing programming and forty-nine private broadcaster affiliates airing varying amounts of that content each day.

As had been the case in the early days of radio, private television stations, expensive to build and operate, found advertising revenue insufficient to maintain a viable business, and a generous subsidy in the form of CBC programming kept many of them in the black while their capital costs were amortized. The economies of scale that a national or even regional network of private TV stations would bring was on the minds of many station owners, but in Ottawa policy-makers saw the role of local stations as filling local needs for non-network programming and advertising.

Other factors mimicked radio's development: viewers along the US border were erecting outdoor yagi antennas and tuning in to American programs in large numbers, and this encouraged a sense of urgency in the need to expand the Canadian system. As well, CBC Television initially carried many programs purchased from the US with a view to weaning Canadian viewers off their America network habits, while introducing them to Canadian content, and, not incidentally, earning substantial advertising revenue for the CBC itself and its revenue-hungry private affiliates.

Television's arrival and the need for regulators and policy-makers to know how to deal with it led Liberal government of Prime Minister Louis St. Laurent to appoint another Royal Commission. Headed by Robert Fowler, president of the Canadian Pulp and Paper Association, the commission reaffirmed the idea of a mixed public-private "single system" operating within defined public-service goals, with the CBC the dominant player. "The choice" according to the commission report, " is between a Canadian state-controlled system with some Canadian content and the development of a Canadian sense of identity, at a substantial public cost, and a privately owned system which the forces of economics will necessarily make predominantly dependent on imported American radio and television programmes."[20] The report also recommended that the task of regulating the industry be taken from the CBC and given to an independent authority, something the CAB and its members had been demanding for decades. "How can we be fairly regulated by a direct competitor?" they wanted to know. Politically, it was a strong argument, though the Fowler

Commission failed to turn up any substantive evidence that the CBC Board of Directors had been anything but scrupulously fair-minded in its regulatory role.

Fowler completed his report in 1957, the year the Progressive Conservative government of Prime Minister John Diefenbaker swept into power in Ottawa. The Conservatives, perennially the CBC's harshest critics in the Commons, passed a new Broadcasting Act the following year which transformed the system, drawing a clear distinction between its public and private sectors, and assigning them different obligations and responsibilities. The new Act placed broadcast regulation in the hands of a separate authority, a newly appointed Board of Broadcast Governors (BBG), which was to oversee separate private and public sectors, placing them for the first time on an equal footing. The legislation bore small resemblance to the spirit or letter of Fowler's recommendations; private broadcasters were delighted.

The CBC's status was further diminished in the new Act by the elimination of funding from license fees on radio and TV receivers.[21] Instead, the public broadcaster would henceforth rely on an annual subsidy granted in principle by Parliament—in fact, by the government of the day. This had the (perhaps unintended) effect of forcing the CBC to pay close attention to developing its advertising income, its only predictable source of revenue. It also meant that the corporation would, in practice and despite its theoretically independent status, be subject to coercion by governments of the day.

PRIVATE SECTOR SUCCESSES

The rapid expansion of private television and the more restrained build-out of CBC facilities through the 1960s was deliberate policy under the Diefenbaker Conservatives, and it would lead to a development that had been deliberately avoided in radio as undermining the "single system" idea—the establishment of private national networks alongside the CBC's. The first private non-CBC-affiliate television licences were issued in 1960 for six cities that already had CBC TV service, and the following year the CTV television network was given the green light by the BBG.[22]

The immediate effect was to steeply increase the amount of American television being consumed by Canadian audiences, since the CTV schedule was heavily weighted to US network content. It also reduced CBC's advertising revenues by twenty percent, and in response the network began a steady shift in its program values toward the commercially successful as opposed to the culturally significant, to satisfy affiliates and to compete for sponsors. Meanwhile revenues for private broadcasters rose from $10 million in 1964 to $22 million a year later, to $100 million by the decade's end. Broadcasting had become the nation's third most profitable industry.

"A new era in broadcasting," rejoiced the *Canadian Broadcaster*. "The CBC has been stopped in its tracks. Its spendings are to be curbed; its monopoly in the TV production field is to be broken; and then, of course, second TV stations are finally on the way." As the CBC was forced through lack of funding to trim back services such as news, professional sports, serious music, drama and public affairs, the magazine said, private stations were positioned to pick up some choice properties.[23]

Graham Spry was deeply disappointed:

> The CBC has been outflanked, surrounded and hemmed in to a subordinate place in the structure of Canadian broadcasting. ... The CBC has been maligned, misrepresented, savaged, nagged and subjected to meanness and indignation by hostile and sometimes greedy competitors and ill-informed politicians. In a generation of conflict between the local private interests ... and the CBC the ordinary forces of money-making have carried the day.[24]

Current figures show that Spry's disappointment was justified. In 2013 the Canadian television industry had grown to more than $17 billion in total revenues, of which only three percent went to the public broadcaster, a number that reflected decades of steady decline in its parliamentary appropriation, accompanied by flat advertising sales on the one hand, and the enormous profitability of the private sector on the other.[25]

At its licence renewal hearings before the CRTC in 1972 the CBC's President Laurent Picard (a Harvard

Ph.D. in business administration) formally announced that the Corporation would in future seek to be more populist in its television programming, opting for what he termed "mass appeal" in a time of expanding viewing options and growing audience fragmentation. By this time, CTV was reaching almost as many Canadian households as CBC Television, and what was to become the Global television network had launched as an Ontario regional superstation. It was at the same licence hearings that the CRTC recommended CBC Television move toward an eventual five-minute-per-hour advertising limit, and that CBC Radio drop commercials altogether. Only the second of these recommendations was acted on; ad revenue on radio was in any case negligible.

Under new presidential leadership in Al Johnson, the CBC continued through the 1970s to struggle with the problem of serving both populist and special-interest audiences on a limited budget, and often failing to do either satisfactorily. In 1980 the corporation released plans for what it saw as the solution: second television networks (CBC-2/Télé-2) that would be non-commercial and feature regionally sourced programming delivered to national audiences, along with programs from the provincial educational channels: the networks would provide second-window viewing opportunities for popular shows from the main channels (current and archived); they would address under-served, specialized audiences for content such as science and technology, business and the economy, culture and the arts. They would provide a venue for experimental new productions, and would air some quality programming purchased abroad. The plan was for these supplementary networks to be delivered directly from CBC studios via satellite to cable companies, for mandatory carriage. They were to be partly financed by a small additional levy on subscribers' monthly bills.

The CRTC turned the plan down; in licence hearings, it had faced a wall of opposition from the cable companies, who had become the regulator's principal clients and who, of course, objected to having to impose new levy on subscriber bills to finance the service. The commission was also aware that Ottawa had been heavily lobbied by proponents of potential private-sector programming initiatives to block any expansion of CBC services.

When the new Trudeau government succeeded the brief interregnum of Joe Clark's Conservatives in 1980, it appointed a commission led by musician Louis Applebaum and writer and journalist Jacques Hébert to revisit the 1951 report of Canada's Royal Commission on National Development in the Arts, Letters, and Sciences (known as the Massey Commission). The Massey report in its comments on the broadcasting industry had been highly critical of interventions it received from private, commercial broadcasters, who complained of having to compete with state-subsidized CBC/Radio-Canada. It noted that the private broadcasters seemed oblivious to "any public responsibility beyond the provision of acceptable entertain-

ment and community services" in their insistence that
that they "must be left free to pursue their business enterprise subject only to limitations imposed by decency and
good taste." The Commission report argued instead that:

> Broadcasting in Canada, in our view, is a
> public service directed and controlled in
> the public interest by a body responsible to
> Parliament. Private citizens are permitted
> to engage their capital and energies in this
> service, subject to the regulation of this
> body. That these citizens should enjoy
> adequate security or compensation for
> the actual monetary investment they are
> permitted to make, is apparent. But that
> they enjoy any vested right to engage in
> broadcasting as an industry, or that they
> have any status except as part of the national
> broadcasting system, is inadmissible. ...
> they have no civil right to broadcast or
> any property rights in broadcasting. They
> have been granted in the national interest a
> privilege over their fellow-citizens.[26]

Like its predecessor, the Applebaum-Hébert report
contained a chapter on broadcasting policy and the CBC;
unlike the Massey report, it recommended the CBC be
dismantled and turned into a program-commissioning
agency for television, selling off its production facilities

to private producers, abandoning all local programming, and confining in-house programming to covering the news.[27] The recommendations were not well-received, either within the CBC or the government, or by the general public. Nevertheless, the notion of directing CBC money to private-sector production houses survived. Famed TV producer Norman Campbell said at the time: "The kind of programs I think are the most interesting to the people of Canada are the kind of shows only the CBC will do. My concern is, if the recommendations go through, I would be very much prevented from doing the kind of show I think people deserve because I think the pressure would be enormous to make these programs international."[28] In 1983 Communications Minister Francis Fox issued a policy directive to the CBC calling for it to begin outsourcing half of its television production to independent firms. The CBC agreed to comply, and a short slide down a slippery slope commenced: today CBC is no longer in the production business, aside from radio and TV news and current affairs. The English language service's historic, irreplaceable costume and set departments were dismantled and sold off in 2007. On the French side, the same thing happened in 2014. CBC Radio shuttered its celebrated drama department in 2012 as a cost-saving measure.

While Applebaum-Hébert was being hotly debated in the press, revolutionary digital compression technologies were spawning another transformation of the media environment. By dramatically lowering the cost of cable and satellite distribution of TV signals (more channels could be pumped down a given cable, or over a satellite transponder), these technological developments made possible an explosion of cable specialty channels. In the ensuing decades the CRTC would award scores of licences for these new channels, almost exclusively to existing commercial broadcasters. Most specialty channels were constructed on platforms already developed by American broadcasters and adapted, with some added Canadian content, to audiences here. HBO was repackaged as HBO Canada; Comedy Central became the Comedy Network; the History Channel became History Television; Bravo became Bravo Canada, and so on. They were expected to be highly profitable because development costs had been largely taken care of in the US, most of the programming was bought at an eighty percent discount, and most of the specialty channels brought in revenue from both advertising and pass-through (licensing) levies paid for by cable subscriber fees.

Thus, while television audiences were badly fragmented by the many new viewing options, owners of both conventional television stations and specialty cable channels were able to reassemble those audiences over multiple platforms. Multimedia conglomerates like Bell Canada, Rogers, Shaw, Astral, and Quebecor discovered that programming could be endlessly cross-promoted across newspaper, magazine, television, radio, and online services. However, these promotional benefits were available only if corporate owners were big enough to assemble a large stable of such services, conventional and digital, capable of pulling together cumulative audiences large enough to interest advertisers; this prompted the scramble of buy-outs and leveraged takeovers that has given Canada's media landscape its current claustrophobic, monopolistic structure.[29]

The CBC was largely sidelined from this transformative development, partly because of its perennial money woes, and partly because of senior management who had little knowledge of the industry, but also because the CRTC refused those applications the CBC did make—eight of them were turned down in the 1990s.[30] (Licences for cable news services in English and French were granted to the CBC in 1987 and 1995, respectively.) Not only was the public broadcaster denied access to the fountain of revenue represented by cable pass-through fees, but it had to cope with exponentially increasing competition for audiences in virtually all genres of programming in this new, highly fragmented universe.

Today, the independent television or radio station is a thing of the past: virtually all broadcast media are owned by the handful of huge corporate entities that also provide subscription television service to Canadians via cable and satellite, as well as telephone and Internet services. The top five of these vertically integrated giants—the CRTC calls them broadcast distribution undertakings, or BDUs—are household names across Canada: Bell Media, Cogeco, Rogers Media, Shaw Media, and Quebecor. Together, they control nearly ninety percent of the media distribution market.

To some, Canada's current media landscape looks like a dangerously concentrated oligopoly. But to others, it speaks of a healthy rationalization and efficient consolidation of assets. It's argued that the "corporatization," "rationalization" and vertical integration of media industries in Canada is a good thing, because it takes radio and television stations, newspapers, and other mass media out of the hands of individuals, and places them under professional, ideologically disinterested, corporate management. It has meant the end of the ego-driven, meddling, media mogul, a figure of privilege prominent in the early history of radio and network television in this country.[31]

But it is patently naive to think that, unlike media moguls of yore, current corporate conglomerates and their managers have no ideological axes to grind, no agenda to push. They do indeed have a shared ideological position, which they promote and defend—the ideology of liberal capitalism. That is, they have an ideological bias against government activism, regulation, and public service beyond the strictures of capitalist orthodoxy that, for example, limit "altruistic" spending to one percent of corporate earnings. And the idea that professional corporate managers are likely to have the expertise needed to support better media performance, from any perspective other than the bottom line, is not supported by the evidence. "Efficient" corporate management has, for example, decimated Canadian news and public affairs operations across media platforms as the growth of the new conglomerates has flourished through the mergers and takeovers of recent decades.[32] The sad fact of corporate media life is that managers have no motivation to improve public service, or the quality of programming, or Canadian content, beyond the minimum that regulation requires and audiences will tolerate, because that would mean wasting money that rightfully belongs to shareholders. It's a well-known axiom that where public-interest regulation and corporations are concerned, minimums become maximums.

This axiom has had ample demonstration in the struggle to provide Canadian content on the nation's media.

CHAPTER 3

CANADIAN CONTENT: A MUTABLE FEAST

The history of radio and television in Canada is in large measure one of preoccupation with the need to ensure listeners and viewers an adequate supply of programming produced by and for Canadians. Nurturing domestic media is a policy objective of many nations, but it was an issue made particularly acute in Canada, by geography: the country's long border with the United States meant that American radio and television signals were able to dominate the Canadian airwaves. The programs were, of course, in English, and they featured the most popular and heavily publicized artists and personalities of their time. Even in Quebec, American media threatened to drown out Canadian voices through sheer mass and amplitude. Simply building more domestic radio and television stations proved to be an insufficient response, since private broadcasters quickly learned that the easiest route to profitability lay in purchasing American programs at fire-sale discounts, filling them with advertising, and re-broadcasting them in prime time to receptive Canadian audiences. It would take a combination of regulatory quotas and richly endowed production funds, backed by an extensive public broadcasting system, to eventually provide a comprehensive, if only partly satisfactory answer.

The Diefenbaker government's broadcast regulator, the BBG, was the first to venture seriously into Can-con territory. To the surprise of many observers at the time, the BBG moved quickly, soon after its establishment in 1958, to impose Can-con rules on the flourishing television industry. It considered a pair of options: reserving two hours of prime time on all private stations as a venue for programs of "public interest and significance" (to be defined by the BBG but presumed to be of Canadian origin); and setting a minimum threshold for Can-con on all stations. The first option would have had the effect of maintaining the spirit of the old single-system, public-service idea, with private stations carrying prime-time programs of "national significance" right across the country, even when there were no willing commercial sponsors. When even the CBC objected to this idea, saying it would give the BBG too much influence over CBC scheduling, the second, quota, approach was adopted with the grudging acceptance of the private industry. The Canadian Association of Broadcasters (CAB) had said publicly it would accept a thirty-five percent Can-con level progressing to forty-five percent over three years, but the BBG shocked them with a fifty-five percent minimum effective in two years. (CBC TV was already filling sixty-five percent of its prime time with Canadian programming.)

Howls of outrage greeted the BBG's Can-con initiative. Advertisers and agencies claimed that the rule would lead to soaring costs and inferior programming. The *Canadian Broadcaster* editorialized that Can-con regulations "would simply give would-be performers without a future a completely false sense of their own abilities." Media mogul Roy Thompson said, "Let's face it, the best American programs are the best in the world. People want to see the best." CAB president Don Jamieson told a Parliamentary broadcasting committee that the Can-con regulations "may give a few second-rate piccolo players or a western band a job [but] the material is just not there."[33] Private broadcasters saw Canadian content as a drain on profit from up-front production expenses and the opportunity costs of airing hard-to-sell Can-con instead of more profitable American programs. Many station owners found ways to fill their Canadian content quotas at minimum cost: broadcaster Ken Soble asked, "Why spend $3,000 or $4,000 when you can get the same credit for hiring a piano player?"[34] This strategy of course helped fulfill the prophecy that the regulations would foster mediocrity. The BBG, for its part, kept the fifty-five percent rule, but watered down the administrative details: during prime time only forty percent Can-con would be required; the definition of Canadian content was broadened to include, for example, speeches by the US President and World Series baseball games.

Even in their diluted form, the BBG's Can-con regulations were not well enforced, and in 1964 the Liberal government of Prime Minister Lester Pearson asked Robert Fowler to once again look into the issue. The opening line of Fowler's report is justly celebrated: "The only thing that really matters in broadcasting is program content: all the rest is housekeeping." He found systematic rule-breaking by private broadcasters: "In fact, the program performance of the private stations ... bears little resemblance to the promises made to the BBG when the licences were recommended." He found a BBG unable to enforce its own rules, since licences were issued by a different government department. "A promise made by a broadcaster to obtain a licence to operate a radio or television station should be an enforceable undertaking, and not a theoretical exercise in imagination or a competitive bid in an auction of unrealistic enthusiasm," his report said.[35]

The Canadian content problem was greatly amplified with the explosion of cable television beginning in the late 1960s, making many more American channels available. (In 1970, eighty percent of Canadian households received their television over the air; by 1978 a majority of homes were receiving their television on cable.) As Fowler noted, the cable industry had been largely unregulated and so in 1968, when the Liberal government of Pierre Trudeau enacted a new Broadcasting Act, this oversight was corrected. The new Broadcasting Act replaced the BBG with a new regulator, the Canadian Radio Television Communication Commission (CRTC). Regulatory responsibilities that had previously been dispersed among several government departments were brought under the control of the new agency, and cable companies were included. For the first time, the broadcast regulator was given the power to issue and withdraw licences for both broadcasters and cable distributors, and to impose "conditions of license" enforceable by strong sanctions up to and including denial of licence renewals. Cable companies launched legal challenges to the regulator's authority over them, losing twice at the Supreme Court of Canada. The courts conceded, however, that the CRTC could not regulate pay-TV services in which the customer pays a subscription fee for delivery of content through a set-top decoder.

THE SIM-SUB BONANZA

The arrival of the CRTC was certainly not all bad news for private broadcasters. In its endeavours to ensure the continuing viability of the Canadian industry, one of the Commission's first acts was to institute a policy known in the business as "sim-sub," which, since 1972, has funnelled enormous sums of money into private television (approximately $250 million a year by current estimates).[36] When a cable company brings a US network signal into Canada for its subscribers, that signal poses a threat to conventional TV stations that have purchased some of the same US network programs with the intention of selling them to Canadian advertisers. These ad sales in US programs form the bulk of most private stations' revenue. To prevent audience-splitting between the domestic broadcaster and US channels carried on cable services from undermining the broadcaster's advertising revenue, the sim-sub regulation imposed by the CRTC specifies that, whenever a cable company is carrying a US program simultaneously from a US source and a Canadian station, the cable company must substitute the Canadian station's signal—along with its Canadian commercials—for the US original. (Thus, Canadian viewers saw the NFL Superbowl with Canadian, not American, commercials, whether or not they selected an American network on their remotes.)

While it was a financial boon for private broadcasters, sim-sub seriously complicated the CRTC's attempts to boost levels of Canadian content, because Canadian television networks have to air their Hollywood-purchased programs simultaneously with the US networks for the benefit to kick in. This leads them to build their schedules around the US prime-time offerings. As a rule, that pretty well fills up peak evening viewing hours, with only off-peak times left over for CRTC-mandated Canadian content. As policy analyst Robert Armstrong observes:

> In an environment of second-best scheduling and limited promotion, it is very difficult for Canadian 'priority' programs with their comparatively limited production budgets (e.g. C$1 million per hour for

drama) to attract audiences comparable to the high-budget U.S programs (e.g. C$3.5 million per hour) with their high-profile stars and media promotion, that are aired on Canadian private sector conventional services.[37]

NEW RULES FOR THE CRTC, CBC

The 1968 Broadcasting Act set out a number of objectives that the CRTC was expected to pursue, based on the underlying idea that broadcasting plays an indispensable role in developing and maintaining Canadian identity. "The Canadian broadcasting system," the Act read, "should be effectively owned and controlled by Canadians so as to safeguard, enrich and strengthen the cultural, political, social and economic fabric of Canada." Where a conflict arose between the objectives of private broadcasters and the objectives of the CBC as set out in the Act, the regulator was expected to resolve it in favour of the CBC.

As revised in 1991, the current Act contains similar wording, and sets out in much the same language the role of the public broadcaster. Section 3 of the Act establishes that the broadcasting system as a whole "shall be effectively owned and controlled by Canadians," and must serve both official languages. All broadcasters should help to "safeguard enrich and strengthen the cultural, political, social, and economic fabric" of the nation. The system should "encourage the development of Canadian expression by providing a wide range of programming that reflects Canadian attitudes, opinions, ideas, values, and artistic creativity." To this end, broadcasters are expected to make "maximum use … of Canadian creative and other resources in creation and presentation of programming." Programming should in general be of "high quality," and it should be "varied and comprehensive, providing a balance of information, enlightenment, and entertainment for men, women, and children of all ages, interests and tastes."[38]

The CBC, as the national public broadcaster, is to provide radio and television services incorporating a wide range of programming that "informs, enlightens and entertains." More specifically, the programming should be "predominantly and distinctively Canadian;" it should "reflect Canada and its regions to national and regional audiences, while serving the special needs of those regions;" its programs should "actively contribute to the flow and exchange of cultural expression." It is also expected to provide programming in French and English that is of "equivalent" quality, paying heed to the special needs of English and French linguistic minorities across the country.[39]

The phrase "predominantly and distinctively Canadian," is echoed in sections of the current, 1991, Act that deal with broadcasters in general, and not just the CBC.[40] Private broadcasters are expected to "contribute in an appropriate manner to the creation and presentation of Canadian programming," phrasing which clearly anticipates that the CRTC will take an active role in defining "appropriate" in the case of individual stations, networks and delivery platforms. Private broadcasters and distributors are required, as well, to "make maximum use, and in no case less than predominant use, of Canadian creative and other resources in the creation and presentation of programming," unless the nature of the service being provided makes this impossible as, for example, in the case of a foreign-language service produced outside Canada.

These are powerful directives in support of Canadian content, and they reflect earlier public policy and legislation all the way back to 1932. However, Can-con regulations have become more controversial with each successive iteration of the Broadcasting Act, because they impose "extraneous" costs on private broadcasters and thus cut into their profits. In the 1970s and 1980s and onward into the current century, neo-liberal attitudes to government intervention replaced the more activist attitudes of the interwar and post-war periods; nevertheless CRTC regulation has managed to maintain minimal levels of Canadian fare on private television, while radio Can-con rules have provided an enormous boon to the domestic music industry.

The CRTC operates as a tribunal: when a need for new policy is identified, it holds public hearings to which interested parties are invited. Members of the public can also make interventions, though this is generally done in writing. Submissions are then analyzed and evaluated (like a court of law, the Commission can only consider the evidence presented to its hearings) and a ruling is made. Soon after his appointment in 1968 as the first CRTC Commissioner, Pierre Juneau and his fellow regulators called hearings that ultimately resulted in the reaffirming of fifty-five percent Can-con minimums for conventional, over-the-air television. In 1970, minimums were raised to sixty percent despite strong objections from the CAB, which called the new rules "the road to Nazism."[41]

After failing to meet its Can-con quota, and receiving only a conditional licence renewal from the CRTC in 1979, CTV took the regulator to court. Following an initial success in Federal Court, the CTV complaint was dismissed by the Supreme Court, which reaffirmed the CRTC's regulatory authority. (Nearly a decade earlier the Senate Committee on Mass Media—the "Davey Committee"—had excoriated private television for airing eighty percent American programming in prime time despite making a before-tax return on equity of fifty percent.)

Canadian content targets for broadcasters and broadcast distribution undertakings such as cable and satellite distributors are implemented through a complex set of administrative definitions and targets that rely on numerical quotas for production ingredients such as authorship, performance venue, copyright ownership, nationality of actors, producers and directors and so on.[42] Recognizing that the production of Canadian content is often an uneconomic proposition, the CRTC, the federal Department of Heritage, and provincial governments have over the years established tax credit schemes and funding agencies to support projects whose producers can meet these numerical targets. To the extent that Can-con can be quantified in these ways, subjective bureaucratic discretion as to worthiness is reduced to a minimum. (It must be noted, however, that reducing any creative project's quality or worthiness to a numerical value is a dubious exercise at best.) For the most part, tax credits are intended to support industrial goals, while funding agencies ostensibly target cultural ends. Foremost among the "cultural" agencies is the Canadian Media Fund, which distributed more than $350 million in production subsidies in 2013 – 2014; the total value of all government subsidies to Can-con across media platforms is more than twice that amount.

There is little question that this money has helped to develop a thriving Canadian production industry. Whether it has significantly boosted production of what most people would recognize as authentic Canadian content on television is far less certain. Much of the money is spent in support of productions aimed at the specialty channel market—cooking, DIY renovation, real-estate, lifestyle and other generic content that is not identifiably Canadian. In 2013 only sixteen percent of the $2.7 billion spent by the Canadian industry on "Canadian" programming went to support what the CRTC defines as programs of national interest, such as dramas, comedies, and documentaries. And because the Media Fund is mandated by the government to focus its attention on financially successful productions, proposals for drama, comedy, and documentary projects are likely to be deliberately cleansed of too much authentically Canadian content, in order to increase the potential for revenue from foreign sales.

The result has been a strong independent production industry that produces little indigenous, authentically Canadian programming—programs that strongly reflect Canadian people, geography, experience, attitudes, history, and values. Profit is maximized in this industry by the production of generic programs that can be easily sold on international markets. The automotive equivalent of these shows would be Ontario-assembled Toyota Corollas. The absence of indigenous content on Canadian screens constitutes a market failure that only a well-funded independent public broadcaster is likely to correct.

In March 2015, the CRTC announced substantial revisions to regulations imposing minimum daily Canadian content quotas of fifty-five percent on conventional television broadcasters. Those quota levels were maintained for weekday prime time (6 to 11 p.m.) but dropped to zero for the rest of the day. Cable specialty channels had their Can-con requirements, which had varied from fifteen to eighty-five percent, harmonized at thirty-five percent. While reducing content quotas, the CRTC retained the spending requirements for Can-con often imposed as a condition of licence, in order to encourage broadcasters to spend more money on fewer programs. The hope was that this would raise the overall volume of high-quality Canadian content on television. It was hoped that broadcasters would end the practice of simply recycling a small backlist of Canadian programs over and over to meet Can-con quotas. The policy change was explicit recognition that previous approaches, while helping to build a thriving production industry, had substantially failed in meeting reasonable benchmarks for high-quality, indigenous Canadian content.

NEW DISTRIBUTION PLATFORMS

In the second decade of the twenty-first century, the broadcasting environment underwent further dramatic changes riding on yet another crest of disruptive technology. This time it wasn't television, or cable, or specialty channels, or digital convergence, or personal video recorders—each a creator of industry havoc in its time. The new disruptor is the rapidly expanding portfolio of services providing video and audio on demand, streamed over the Internet to home and portable devices. Netflix, Songza, and their many imitators are changing the ways in which we consume television and radio. The popularity of this so-called "over-the-top" or OTT delivery model is growing fast: between 2008 and 2014 average weekly viewing hours of Internet television had quintupled, to more than five hours. Conventional television viewing, meanwhile, remained static at just under thirty hours a week. OTT usage gains reflect a starting point of zero, and will eventually plateau; the crucial questions are at what level, and will OTT eventually begin to pull down conventional cable satellite and over-the-air viewing.

In this climate of uncertainty, the dilemma facing the CRTC is whether, and how, to regulate OTT services. Just as there was for early radio, and then television, and then cable, there is a clear need with OTT to correct for market failure: the failure of the unregulated market to provide adequate public service in the form of support for bona fide Canadian cultural goals. Netflix, for example, pulls more than $100 million in subscriber revenues out of Canada each year in direct competition with conventional television and cable operations. And yet it is unregulated—it pays no money into any Canadian media development fund to support Canadian content, nor does it promise to carry any minimum level of Canadian programming in its catalogue. This would be less worrisome if it were not the case that some variation of the Netflix model appears likely to dominate in the industry over the next ten years or so. In a country where domestic content has for many decades been made available through a system of regulated minimum Can-con carriage requirements on the demand side, and, on the supply side, a system of direct subsidies to producers and broadcasters, OTT regulation is a serious issue. How can the production, distribution, and consumption of quality Canadian programming be assured when so much video content— mostly American for now, but increasingly from all over the world— is available via the Internet, delivered by distributors that are beyond the reach of Canadian regulators?

Whether the CRTC has legal authority to regulate

programming delivered via the Internet is an open question. Much depends on how the Broadcasting Act's definition of "broadcasting" is interpreted. The Commission itself maintains that it does have the authority to regulate media delivered via the Internet, but has chosen, while technologies are in flux, not to exercise it. The issue will only be resolved by a court challenge, or a new Broadcasting Act. Whatever happens, it will remain the case that the market failures exhibited by the broadcasting industry are no less evident in the new world of online delivery platforms like Netflix, YouTube and Shomi than they ever were, and therefore the rationale for regulation imposing Can-con limits is no less valid than it was in 1932, or 1936, or 1968, or 1991. Whatever the platform, the unfortunate fact remains that it is simply unprofitable to produce Canadian content in a market awash in cheap American programming options.

The drift to ubiquitous, difficult-to-regulate OTT television only reinforces the fact that the only reliable way to provide authentic Canadian content for Canadian audiences, on any platform, is to produce it in adequate quantity through the auspices of a well-funded, well-managed public broadcaster dedicated to that task. In a multi-platform universe, the role of the CBC/Radio-Canada is more important than ever.

CHAPTER 4

PUBLIC BROADCASTING AS AN IDEAL

The ability to transmit sound and images via radio waves is a blend of scientific and entrepreneurial genius, one of the modern industrial era's most remarkable innovations. The subsequent invention of public broadcasting, a creation of politicians and public servants, is arguably an achievement of equal significance. The decision to forge a new and potentially lucrative communication technology into a free and universal public amenity was both inspired and courageous. It was a product of men and women whose values had roots in the refined sensibilities of the *belle époque* in Europe, and the civic duty ethic of Victorian England; and the recent catastrophe of World War I had taught them how fragile civilization can be.

We owe the creation of public-service broadcasting in its purest form to Great Britain and the British Broadcasting Corporation. The purpose of the BBC, according to

its founding director John Reith, was to "inform, educate, and entertain," in that order of priority. Contained
in this extraordinary mission statement, which dates from
1924, are the two most important defining characteristics of public-service media: as near to universal access
as is possible; and the highest attainable quality of content, in whatever genre. Universal access is taken to mean
that where you live, how well educated you are, or how
much you earn, should not lead to disenfranchisement.
The logic of universal accessibility is not of maximizing
audience, but of equal rights. The issue of quality is more
complex, and will be dealt with it in detail later on in this
chapter. However, for the moment it is important to note
that quality speaks to universality as well. For the programming output of a public broadcaster to be considered
of high quality, it must be more than just well made; it
must appeal to a broad range of tastes and interests.

The British media scholar Michael Tracey has put it
this way:

> Public broadcasting does not expect that it can
> please all of the people all of the time—indeed
> it sees in that approach precisely the kind of
> populism which nurtures cultural mediocrity,
> as quality is sacrificed on the altar of
> maximizing audience size. Public broadcasting
> does, however, believe that well-produced
> programmes can please a lot of the people a
> lot of the time, and everybody some of the

time. Public broadcasting is thus driven by the desire to make good programmes popular and popular programmes good: it understands that serving national diversity is not the same as "giving people what they want.[43]

Serving diversity means catering to tastes from popular to elite. One of public broadcasting's values is that, in doing so, it can hope to stir a latent interest or revive a dormant passion in some segment of the audience. It extends cultural horizons by offering audiences not only what they want, but what they may not yet know they want.

Public broadcasting is also in a unique position to provide programming for ethnic, cultural, gender, and minority interests, as well as for children. It is especially useful to the socially and physically disadvantaged. These are groups which almost by definition are neglected by commercial media, which see audience maximization in affluent demographics as a crucial business imperative. Public broadcasting can both help minorities communicate with one another and bring their interests to the attention of a wider public.

The educational part of public broadcasting's mandate has both formal and informal aspects. The CBC has for the past several decades neglected the formal approach, acknowledging (or rationalizing) that education is a provincial responsibility under the Canadian constitution. Education has been downloaded to provincial public-service broadcasters, where they exist (although recently the CBC has been expanding educational resources on its Web portal, cbc.ca).[44] There is no CBC counterpart, for example, to the BBC-supported Open University, which offers about 600 courses leading to 250 formal academic qualifications, including post-graduate university degrees.

Finally, it is an axiom of public broadcasting that it should be free from the influence of vested interests, be they state or commercial, or even philanthropic. Programs paid for by advertisers inevitably have their content shaped by the business imperative of broadening the audience base, and by the values inherent in consumer culture. On the other hand, programs directly financed by the state, without the intervening buffers afforded by institutional structures such as an autonomous Crown Corporation, and arm's-length funding, will inevitably reflect political interests. And finally, philanthropists, too, give their money to causes they believe in and are comfortable with, which is not always where the need is; the process is undemocratic. In each case, he who pays the piper calls the tune.

But the independence required of true public broadcasting is more than simple insulation from political and pecuniary influences. It must also be morally independent. It must be free to explore, reflect, and criticize the values of both governments and commercial interests, and of communities to which it broadcasts. In this respect, the public broadcaster must be afforded the same kind of intellectual independence as a university.[45]

SERVING TWO MASTERS

The CBC has throughout its history been subject to more or less continuous attack from private broadcasting interests and their lobbyists in Ottawa, who have objected to competition from a publicly funded institution.[46] Adding their voices to the chorus more recently have been neoliberal ideologues, who see state-subsidized enterprises of any kind as market-distorting abominations. A succession of federal governments have for eighty years and more made mollifying compromises that have left the public broadcaster in an ambiguous, confused, and ultimately untenable position, scrambling to maintain mandated services with grossly inadequate resources.

In its efforts to stay afloat, the CBC has at times seemed wildly schizophrenic, a symptom of the contradiction inherent in its heavy reliance on television advertising to supplement a dwindling parliamentary appropriation. CBC Radio was set free from commercial sponsors in 1974—and subsequently flourished— but since its inception, CBC Television has been financed in part by advertising, a source of revenue that becomes more important with each successive reduction in the federal government subsidy. Until the NHL hockey franchise was lost to Rogers Media in 2014, advertising had provided roughly a third of the network's income, and was considered critical to its survival. Without revenue from hockey, the Corporation's advertising revenue fell from $245 million in 2011 – 2012 to about $100 million, which, according to one knowledgeable source, is not much more than the cost of maintaining its sales department.[47]

With one foot in the altruistic ethic of public service and the other in market values, CBC Television has had to cope with conflicting mandates arising out of what media scholar Graham Murdock identifies as "a sharp distinction between those programs that people in their role as consumers of television most enjoy and those that, as citizens, they value for their contribution to the overall quality of public life."[48]

This distinction is reflected in two radically different notions of what constitutes the public interest. The market model of media defines serving the public interest as "giving the public what it wants." A large audience is therefore a sign that the public interest is being served— otherwise those people would be doing something else. The theory further suggests that in a democratic society the state or its representatives have no right to make choices for citizens as to what they can watch or listen to, any more than what they read or write. Therefore, any definition of the public interest other than its own is antidemocratic.

A public-service model, on the other hand, tends to put some distance between the audience and the programmers, in the sense that program decisions are not made solely on the basis of past experience with audience response. This approach concerns itself with what listeners and viewers *ought* to be interested in, what they are *capable* of appreciating and enjoying, and what is likely to enrich rather than impair their lives, not just what audiences have already demonstrated an interest in. It leaves space, in other words, for the audience to be surprised, and for tastes and interests to be developed. The focus of the public-service model is on the kind of programming that is intended to inform, edify and entertain, but also to promote the public good by illuminating issues and promoting engaged and active cultural and political citizenship. The idea is that the state, in one way or another, should ensure that there is a depth, diversity, quality, and independence of media content that market forces alone will not supply. Of course there is nothing to say that programs cannot serve both market and public-service interests at the same time, as they sometimes do on CBC Television, and frequently do on European public broadcasters.

There is something about the word ought, italicized in the paragraph above, that raises peoples' hackles when it's applied to the media. Public broadcasting is often accused of being elitist because it dares to make such judgments about what's worthy of attention. But this is a misrepresentation, or at least an unfairly narrow interpretation, of what public broadcasting aims to do. It does not aim to force anything down peoples' throats; it strives instead to extend people's range of choices, and engage them willingly with content of a kind they are unlikely to find on any commercially sponsored outlet.

And as to elitism, it's worth remembering that *all* radio and television programming, whether commercial or public-interest, is provided by elites in the sense of well-educated, highly skilled cadres with privileged access to powerful technologies. In broadcasting, somebody else decides what you watch or listen to, and you have very little say in the matter. You can, in the idiom, "vote with the remote," but your freedom to choose is confined to the menu presented to you in the TV and radio listings. And while the menu may be vast, multiplicity is no guarantee of diversity.

Who draws up the menu? Commercial media are programmed by an elite group of producers, mainly in Hollywood, who are skilled in deciding what will interest audiences and serve the needs of advertisers, while at the same time earning a healthy profit for the producers and distributors. They work in collaboration with advertisers and their representatives to ensure that commercials will integrate well with the overall package, and the right audience demographics will be addressed. Thus the choices offered by commercial media fall—*must* fall—within narrowly prescribed boundaries of what is compatible with sponsors' messages. They must not seriously conflict with the conventions and ideological themes of consumerism and liberal market capitalism. And they must not be challenging or disturbing enough to make the advertisements that surround them seem crass or in poor taste. The commercial media elite, to the extent that they are successful, are highly skilled in navigating this landscape.

Public-service media are programmed by a different kind of elite, by groups of men and women who are expected to devote themselves to serving the public interest. Like their colleagues employed by commercial media interests, they constitute a small, highly specialized and skilled centre of power and influence. But they are in principle free to develop programming that stretches the imagination and challenges the intellect while entertaining and informing the audience. They can take creative risks no rational commercial broadcaster could countenance. They can produce documentary programming few advertisers would want to sponsor. They can spend money on honing quality beyond the point of optimum cost-to-audience-retention formulae.

So the question becomes: which elite do you prefer to provide your media content? It needn't be one or the other; most of us like some of each. But few thoughtful people would choose to rely on the commercial elite exclusively. Polling bears this out: Canadians over the years have consistently and by overwhelming margins ranked the CBC's contribution to Canadian culture as either "important" (more than fifty percent) or "very important" (more than thirty percent).[49]

THE BBC'S EVOLUTION

The notion of public-service broadcasting as it has been understood at the BBC has evolved over time. It begins with John Reith's famous injunction, worth repeating here, that public radio should "bring into the greatest possible number of homes … all that is best in every department of human knowledge, endeavour, and achieve-

ment."[50] The intent, a noble one, was Victorian in its paternalism. To educate and elevate tastes was the purpose
of the BBC, and the reason why it had to be a monopoly:
competition, and in particular commercial competition,
would eventually result in broadcasters giving their audiences (who were presumed to be poor judges of what was
good for them) merely what they wanted. Broadcasting,
Reithian style, was a benevolent project in top-down social engineering. His loyal successor as Director-Gener-
al, William Haley, described the mission in a talk on the
BBC Home Service in 1949 as "the disinterested search
for the Truth," adding that "it should be frankly stated
that to raise standards is one of the purposes for which the
BBC counts." It must do this, however—and this was an
important nuance—"within the broad contract that the
listener must be entertained ... [so that] while giving him
the best of what he wants, it tries to lead him to want
something better."[51]

In a prescient comment that foreshadows the debate
over our present state of media saturation and civic disen-
gagement, Haley insisted that broadcasting should be seen
as an intermediary between the individual and the world
of everyday experience, so that properly done, it would
lead people to real-life experiences such as the theatre,
concert hall, town hall meeting, or election rally. The
aim of broadcasting "must be to make people active, not
passive, both in the fields of recreation and public affairs.
... The wireless set or the TV receiver are only signposts
on the way to a full life. That must finally lie in a sense

of beauty and joy in all things, and in the experience of participating in life as a whole."[52]

The challenge that preoccupied these early leaders of public broadcasting was expressed neatly by Harman Grisewood, a famous BBC actor, staff announcer, and eventually director of the high-brow Third Programme (a third radio network) on the BBC: "How are we to ensure the continuity of our culture in an age of mass participation?" The culture he had in mind was one that had been described by Haley in 1946 as founded on "the things that matter ... the ancient moral values" that "derive from Greece, Rome and the Holy Land ... [forming] the basis of our civilization."[53]

This outlook strikes the contemporary Canadian's ear as quaint or even outrageous in its parochialism, as does Reith's paternalistic, classist authoritarianism. As British society went through the wrenching post-war transformations brought about by massive immigration, the rise of consumerism, the market's unrelenting preaching of self-interest and individualism, and the relativism and skepticism of newly fashionable postmodern philosophy, the old model was challenged. The public broadcaster's function might still be to serve the public good, but it was no longer clear what "good" looked like.

Throughout the 1950s and 1960s the BBC was faced with new social realities and with a rising tide of commercial, for-profit competition, first from Europe and then at home. It struggled to find the sweet spot between elite and populist tastes. A 1957 internal inquiry into how the corporation ought to respond acknowledged that "the loss of its monopoly in broadcasting has very much reduced the BBC's power to manipulate its programme policy in the interest of social and cultural aims," adding: "It is instead engaged in a battle for its position as the nation's home entertainer, a position it must retain if it is to continue as the mirror of the nation's great events and a cultural and educational influence of social importance." Commercial populism had effectively gained the upper hand. The BBC would henceforth be obliged to service its many audiences "more as it finds them than as it would wish them to be."[54] The question now became whether or not that need necessarily led to a lowering of standards or a betrayal of the broadcaster's original public purpose and high ideals.

The internal logic of the continuing renewal process at the BBC would eventually produce one of the corporation's most successful Directors General, Hugh Greene. Greene's vision for the BBC rested on the need to continue its traditional mode of financing through a license fee on radio and television sets, in order to maintain both its arm's-length relationship to government and its commercial-free programming schedule. Even minimal commercial financing would, he said, be a slippery slope: "If we were successful in the commercial field there would be inevitable political pressure to deprive us of our license revenue, gradually but in the end totally."[55]

Commercial broadcasting, Greene said, was characterized by salesmanship rather than service, "the mere desire to attract attention" by any means. "I believe the profit-servicing system is defective. Its interests can never be towards providing the best in every category—its concern is fundamentally with sales and its categories of broadcasting are categories of salesmanship." Not only were commercial broadcasters obliged to tailor programs to suit advertisers, the ratings-based measurement of their worth "is bound to be a deceptive and specious one." Why? Because the requirements of public service, he said,

> are as manifold and diverse as the individuals who compose the public. A library considered as a public service could hardly be correctly evaluated merely in terms of the number of books borrowed. If this were the standard of measurement, libraries would have a very easy road, and we could easily guess at what the contents of this library would be. But a public service of broadcasting, like the library, must provide so far as possible for every taste and for every sort of entertainment, for information upon every worthwhile topic, and for education wherever it is needed.[56]

Whatever the public broadcaster does, Greene insisted, must be informed by civic rather than commercial values, and if some saw that as paternalism, then so be it. He said in a speech to the National Association of Adult Education in 1961: "I hope I shall not sound 'undemocratic' if I say that by and large it is fairly well agreed in our society that knowledge is better than ignorance, tolerance than intolerance, and active concern for the arts or public affairs better than indifference, and that wide interests are better than narrow."

The BBC's current mission statement sums up the public-service broadcaster (PSB) ethic nicely: the broadcaster's programs should "inform, educate, entertain, and enrich the lives of audiences in ways which the market alone will not; bring people together for moments of celebration, common experience, and in times of crisis; and help broaden people's horizons."

VIRTUOUS CIRCLES

There is an aspect of public-service broadcasting both as an ideal and as it is put in practice around the world that does not get the attention it deserves, and that is the role it plays in helping to develop commercial media. Public broadcasting historically has been cast in the role of illegitimate (because subsidized) competitor with, and burden upon, the private broadcasting industry, a complaint heard nowhere more loudly or persistently than in Canada. And yet, there is no denying that in Canada the success of private, commercial broadcasting owes an enormous debt to the assistance it received from the public broadcaster in the industry's early, exploratory days in both radio and television. The many private CBC-affiliate stations benefitted from access to high-quality CBC-produced and -purchased programming, and from CBC's many innovations in broadcast engineering. Even today, the existence of CBC/Radio-Canada takes some of the heat off private broadcasters where the issue of Canadian content is concerned, partially papering over the yawning gap left by the Can-con market failure.

A study produced for Reuters and the BBC Trust by economist Mariana Mazzucato challenges the "crowding out" argument used against public-service broadcasters. In examining historical industry data, she concludes that "there are many parts of the risk landscape where private business fears to tread, so that public investment does not crowd out but *crowds in* private sector investment through its 'de-risking' activity." This is especially true, her research shows, in areas of rapid technological change, like broadcasting. "The BBC is the dynamic element of the UK's creative industry—the catalyst that directly or indirectly generates the chemical reaction that makes private companies (incumbents and indies) invest in risky innovative enterprises."

Mazzucato reports that "crowding in" is true in terms of both programming and technology. Much of the BBC's technical innovation is open-source, so that others in the industry can add their own contributions to development of untried, leading-edge innovations. But the BBC also holds a portfolio of 134 patents on technologies such as its Radioplayer and Stagebox Internet-based multi-camera HD production software, which generate revenue from third-party licences. In terms of program production, the BBC, like most other true public broadcasters, invests in developing small enterprises and promising individuals, often playing the role of business angel. As an example, Mazzucato reports that in 2008 the BBC acquired a twenty-five percent stake in the UK independent producer Big Talk Productions, funding it with further £1,125,000 in loans. The company went on to generate revenues of £11 million in 2011, and received the UK's highest industry award for its situation comedy series *Rev* (aired on BBC Two). BBC international co-productions for television also generated £32 million in foreign direct investment in the UK in 2011. Overall, it is estimated that the public's return on its investment in the BBC is about two to one in terms of economic value, including stable, well-paying jobs.

From the early days of radio in the 1920s the CBC has played a similar role in Canadian broadcasting, leading technological development, sharing it with private broadcasters, and blazing a trail in program innovation. Historically, the Canadian public has invested billions of dollars in production support and technology transfer to the private industry, in the name of building a viable continent-spanning broadcasting system. But those kinds of initiatives have been virtually eliminated in recent decades through successive funding cuts and short-sighted management. Governments today prefer to support the private industry more directly through subsidies in the form of program development funds, tax breaks, and cross-border advertising restrictions. These amount to about $1 billion a year, on a par with the CBC's ever-diminishing federal appropriation.

There is in fact compelling evidence that wherever in the world strong public broadcasters exist, they help create a flourishing private broadcasting sector. A recent study drawing on a wide range of data from sixteen countries was designed to test competing theories about public-service broadcasting frequently heard in debates over the relevance of these services, in Canada and around the world.[57] One theory is that public broadcasters, whatever their virtues, damage commercial broadcasters operating in the same markets by "crowding out" private investment and innovation (examined in the UK context by Mazzucato, above). The second is that public broadcasters have just the opposite effect, creating a market environment in which their commercial counterparts tend to thrive, both financially and in terms of their program quality.

Canada was not included in the study, because the CBC's hybrid public/commercial television system could not accurately be compared with the true public broadcasters like those in the Nordic countries, the UK, Australia, Germany, France and other European and South American nations, which have no commercial sponsorship and operate on state subsidies of one kind or another.

The results were convincing: in assessing the vitality of both public and private broadcasters based on several criteria including revenues and program quality, the health of the private sector was found to be directly and positively correlated with the health of the public broadcaster. That is, the larger and stronger the PSB, the healthier the private sector broadcasters were. This was true in all countries examined, with the single exception of the US, where public-service broadcasting has little government support and holds a tiny share of the enormous domestic broadcasting market, the world's richest.

"On each assessment criteria," the report found, "strong public broadcasting correlates positively with a strong commercial market":

- in countries where funding for public broadcasting is strong, commercial revenues invariably are also strong;
- in countries where the PSB invests heavily in original programming, so does the commercial sector, which strengthens the production market;
- in countries where the PSB offers a wide diversity of program genres, so does the commercial sector, which enhances public service across the board;
- where audience perceptions of quality in PSB television offerings were high they were also high for commercial broadcasting, indicating higher quality.

In the words of the report, "this research supports the theory that public broadcasters drive a virtuous circle by raising audience expectations of all broadcasters, requiring commercial broadcasters to invest in diverse, high-quality output and thereby further challenging PSBs to raise their game."

The audience perception data that was collected showed that in each of the sixteen countries, audiences judged their public broadcaster's programming to be of higher quality than that of commercial broadcasters. But the data also showed that the higher the approval ratings for the PSBs, the higher they were for the commercial broadcasters' output, another indicator of a virtuous circle at work, in which commercial broadcasters strive to meet benchmarks established by the PSBs.

Far from crowding out private enterprise, healthy public broadcasters help generate a strong market ecology in which both the PSBs and the commercial broadcasters are rewarded in audience numbers and appreciation and, for the commercial operators, in strong revenues.

Problems arise, however, when the public broadcaster is also a commercial broadcaster, as in the case of the CBC.

CHAPTER 5

THE CBC AS COMMERCIAL BROADCASTER

The 1991 Broadcasting Act drafted by the Conservative government of Prime Minister Brian Mulroney is the most recent major revision of broadcast policy in Canada, and remains in force at this writing. A year after its adoption, the world's first commercial Internet service provider, The World, set up shop in Brookline, Massachusetts. Two years after that the World Wide Web launched, and Mosaic, the first graphical interface Web browser, was released. The Act was four years old when Amazon.com began selling books online, launching the world of online commerce. The first digital personal video recorder, TiVo, went on sale six years after the Act was passed, and a year later Google was incorporated. It is safe to say that none of this technological development was foreseen by the legislators back in 1991. However, they do seem to have anticipated rapid technological change as the new norm, and the core principles of Canadian broadcasting policy were set out clearly, with the expectation that they would be applied to new platforms and business models as they emerged.

Where it concerns the CBC, the Act is more specific in its expectations. The public broadcaster's programs should be "predominantly and distinctively Canadian," and should "reflect Canada and its regions to national and regional audiences, while serving the special needs of those regions." It should "strive to be of equivalent quality in English and French," and "contribute to shared national consciousness and identity," and at the same time "reflect the multicultural and multiracial nature of Canada." A nod was given to the inevitability of technological change in a clause that instructs the public broadcaster to make its programming "available throughout Canada by the most appropriate and efficient means and as resources become available for the purpose."

These marching orders are broad enough to leave much room for interpretation by CBC/Radio-Canada managers struggling to cope with recurrent budget cuts imposed by a succession of both Conservative and Liberal governments. But the strategy adopted in response to cuts imposed by the deficit-busting Liberal government of Paul Martin in 2004 was a game-changer. A new management team assembled by President Robert Rabinovitch, a Ph.D. in economics and finance, adopted a new approach that involved an all-out attempt to maximize advertising revenue on television. The transformation of CBC Television that followed has been documented in meticulous detail by its principal instigator, Richard Stursberg, the former head of the Canadian Cable Television Association, hired by Rabinovitch.[58]

During his six-rear reign as head of English-language programming, from 2004 to 2010, Stursberg was a staunch champion of catering to populist tastes. During his tenure, talk of public-service mandates was explicitly banned. "We did not want to produce university lectures, books or performing arts.... We wanted to work within the television conventions that English Canadians preferred. We would jettison 'edgy,' auteur-driven projects for season-long series working within understood narrative traditions. We would make police procedurals, situation comedies, reality eliminations, lifestyle shows, and quiz shows. We wanted to make TV for the largest possible audience."[59]

One of Stursberg's first actions in developing a new, advertiser-friendly schedule was to cancel the multiple-award-winning *Opening Night*, two hours of prime time, advertising-free performances broadcast each Thursday evening. "There were plays, ballet one-person shows— beautiful performances. The shows were made to a high standard. The audiences were dismal ... the CBC could not afford to give up the most important [ratings] evening of the week to a show that generated no revenue and rarely made 200,000 viewers. Whether we liked it or not, and despite how beautiful the shows were, Canadians were saying no."[60]

Stursberg's approach marked a radical departure from the traditional public broadcasting ethic, which involved serving, to the extent that it was feasible, all tastes and interests, including niche and specialized areas such as the arts, that private broadcasters either would not or could not address. Stursberg was intent on catering only to the most populist appetites, that is, the audience already being served by commercial broadcasters. He was openly disdainful of anything else, believing that television failed whenever it strayed from the conventions of American network programming. "Television is fundamentally about entertainment. It is the medium par excellence that people consume to be told stories, to be made to laugh, to be thrilled, frightened, moved, charmed or excited." Therefore, to "suggest that the CBC should make shows that were alien to what Canadians knew and liked seemed almost perverse."[61]

By defining CBC Television as a vehicle "fundamentally about entertainment," Stursberg was describing, not the nature of the medium, but the condition of American television. Canadian broadcasting policy is largely a means of overcoming that condition, and the CBC is specifically charged with the responsibility to not only entertain, but also to inform and enlighten. The conventions of American network television, so familiar to Canadians and developed over decades of experimentation, have nothing to do with the nature of the medium and everything to do with the needs of advertisers to keep audiences in an appropriate frame of mind to tolerate and absorb commercials. Stursberg was simply wrong in his conviction that television is fundamentally incapable of taking audiences beyond Hollywood orthodoxy. Even American subscription TV (Showtime, HBO) offers overwhelming contradictory evidence, not to mention the daily output of the world's public broadcasters.[62] Nor are audiences naturally or innately predisposed to love Hollywood-style narrative. It is their preference because it is comfortable and familiar. The television audience in North America has for half a century been purposefully groomed to accept the programs they watch in the absence of fare that might be more challenging, or disturbing, or thoughtful, or inspiring, or enlightening, or relevant to their lives. That's because advertisers, who pay the bills, demand audiences of a particular demographic, and of maximum size, and "mainstream" programming is most cost-effective in assembling those audiences. In the stacks of any university library are shelves of volumes on precisely the problem of Hollywood's product overwhelming, and ultimately changing, local cultural preferences by sheer weight of exposure. It is a theme central to the study of globalization.

Stursberg apparently saw no problem with commercial sponsorship on public television. (Nor, one must assume, did his superior, Robert Rabinovitch.[63]) In his memoir, he never questions its appropriateness. The idea of divided allegiances does not occur to him. In fact, he prides himself in having encouraged the CBC's sales department to promote the public broadcaster as the place to go, not just for conventional spot advertising, but for the more devious rewards of product placement—advertising by stealth. He writes:

> In thinking about revenues we knew we had
> certain advantages over our competitors
> at CTV and Global. Whereas they bought
> most of their shows ready-made in the
> United States, we commissioned or
> produced most of ours from scratch, which
> meant that we could incorporate advertisers
> and sponsors directly into the shows as they
> were being produced. We could do product
> placements, Website extensions or games
> and contests that were integral to the shows
> themselves and helped to sell the sponsors'
> products. Advertisers were happy to pay
> a premium for that, and our competitors
> could not match it.[64]

Some would see this as a stunning betrayal of the public trust. In what conceivable interpretation of the public interest, or the CBC's Broadcast Act mandate, is it acceptable for a public broadcaster to offer up its programs to advertisers for purposes of selling their products subliminally?

In his memoir, *The Tower of Babble: Sins, Secrets and Successes Inside the CBC*, Stursberg waxes enthusiastic: "One of the best examples of how this could be done was *Kraft Hockeyville*," he boasts. *Hockeyville* was a heavily promoted reality show concocted by Stursberg's programmers in which small-town Canada competed for corporate-donated prizes by affirming their devotion to hockey—a sport which, not incidentally, filled about 350 advertising-laden hours on CBC Television each year until 2014. Stursberg continues: "In the show and the online voting, Kraft was woven into everything. *Hockeyville* appeared on Kraft products in supermarkets, and everybody was pleased. To extend the idea further, we commissioned an episode of *Little Mosque on the Prairie* for Kraft.... In this particular episode we had Mercy [the fictional Saskatchewan town in which *Little Mosque* is set] apply to be named *Hockeyville*." He concludes: "In 2008 and 2009 *Marketing* magazine named CBC 'Media Player of the Year' for its innovations. That had never happened before."[65] *Little Mosque* also featured product placement in a deal with TD Bank in 2009 (a character visits a branch to see if he has enough money to throw a party), and in *Being Erica*, a lead character was given the job of manager of a TD bank branch. The bank also appeared by stealth in *Heartland*. Worse, in 2010 CBC teamed up with Kellogg to promote Eggo Waffles with the CBC children's programming puppet character Mamma Yamma.[66] Since the departure of Stursberg the corporation has stopped announcing its product-placement deals in press releases.

It's worth noting, parenthetically, that paid product placement was permitted for the first time on British commercial television by industry regulator Ofcom only in 2011. At the BBC, the ban continues. Under the new regulation, commercial stations must display the letter P at the top right corner of the screen for three seconds at the beginning and end of a program that contains product placement. As well, Ofcom ruled, the placement must not interfere with the editorial content of the program, nor be too prominent. And a total ban remains in place for children's programs, news and current affairs programs, and for alcohol, tobacco, medicines, escort services and products that are high in sugar, salt and fat.[67]

The story does not end there. In response to the financial crunch that faced the CBC in 2009 (brought on by the Great Recession and resultant drop-off in advertising revenue), Stursberg proposed that "we should jettison the block of pre-school shows for children in the mornings." The CBC, like all other public broadcasters, had always considered children's programming to be absolutely central to the fulfillment of its public-service mandate. The quality of CBC's children's programming had earned a world-wide reputation, and programs like *The Friendly Giant* had imprinted themselves on the Canadian psyche. But Stursberg had noticed that they "carried no advertising and had very small audiences."[68] At the same time he asked the CBC Board of Directors to reverse the corporation's long-standing policies banning infomercials and political advertising outside election periods. Both requests were denied.[69]

Stursberg was dismissed by incoming president Hubert Lacroix in 2010. His legacy lives on, however, and since that time, he has continued to promote his vision of a CBC that leads the ratings in populist programming at the expense of every other genre, claiming that, thanks to his visionary strategy, "it is possible to say with cer-

tainty that the CBC has never been stronger." Writing in
The Globe and Mail two years after his dismissal, Stursberg
claimed that, thanks to his leadership, "for the first time
in history, the CBC has proven that Canadians can make
entertainment shows that can compete with the programs
made in the United States.... If there ever was a Golden
Age for the CBC, it is now." (The facts tell a different
story: Canadians' average weekly viewing hours of CBC
Television *fell* from 43.3 to 27.6 between 2009 and 2013.[70])

Many Canadians, including legions of loyal CBC Radio addicts, see in the television service what *Globe and
Mail* television critic John Doyle sees: "A blinding sheen
of lightweight nonsense." A schedule, punctuated by ratings-grabbing gimmicks like *Battle of the Blades*, in which
"there isn't a single serious-minded cable-quality drama
… a single searing comedy … nothing to compel anyone
to note that no other broadcaster would air such a program."[71] Recent additions to the lineup like the sitcom
Schitt's Creek and a sci-fi adventure series called *Ascension*
have done nothing to change this picture. The CBC's flagship TV newscast *The National* Doyle harpoons in the same
column as "sometimes a disgrace, a meandering journey
through the mind of a flibbertigibbet who spent the day
garnering news bits from a hodgepodge of online sources."

Obviously, Doyle and Stursberg have radically different definitions of successful public broadcasting. Doyle
argues that "the CBC is mandated to be more than a
broadcaster. It is mandated to be a cultural institution, an
incubator of artistic talent, employer of talent from many

genres and provider of unique programming that other broadcasters fail to deliver." For Doyle, the CBC must broaden public taste, rather than pander to it—to provide a venue for excellence. Success is, or ought to be, measured in that context.

For Stursberg and his supporters, success for the CBC has a different meaning. As he makes clear in his memoir, television is not a medium—ever—for high artistic expression, but rather for mass entertainment. He subscribes to the attitude, popular in the commercial media industry, that the success of a television offering is quantifiable in the utilitarian arithmetic of ratings, and that any discussion of quality that does not take place in the context of popularity is simply specious. Viewers choose to watch elimination reality TV shows in large numbers because it is quality television: how do we know it is quality television? By Stursberg's logic, because viewers watch in large numbers.

There is nothing subtle about Stursberg's view. In describing his strategy for renovating CBC Television in *Tower of Babble*, he writes there would be only one measure for success: audiences. "It would be a brutal standard. ... It would no longer allow [the corporation] to fudge the meaning of success by talking vaguely about 'mandates,' and 'quality.' It would be a standard by which shows, producers, stars and executives would be judged."[72]

RATINGS VERSUS QUALITY

At first blush, the ratings-centered approach to measuring success for CBC Television seems eminently sensible. As Stursberg asks, "If not audiences, then what?"[73] And indeed, if the ratings services in which he placed his faith and to which he off-loaded responsibility for quality evaluation truly measured audiences, then Stursberg's position would be more difficult to dismiss. But the fact is that ratings do not really measure audiences in any reasonable or reliable fashion. They provide little or no information as to whether viewers were bored or entranced, stimulated or maddened, inspired or nauseated, made joyful or angry, educated or misled. In short, they offer no clue as to whether the audience has been satisfied or the public interest served. They simply provide an indication of how many warm bodies were located in front of television sets tuned to a particular item on the menu of programs placed on offer by the TV industry. Audiences are composed of real people; ratings, on the other hand, are a completely artificial statistical construct designed to do the impossible—to make a homogeneous, packageable commodity out of millions of individual consumers whose tastes, needs, and responses are unique, and who are as diverse as their numbers.

Ratings say nothing coherent about whether the audience is being well served. Then why do they exist? Because markets, which are the means through which commodities are distributed in an economy, run on numbers. In the peculiar market that is commercial television, the commodity being sold by broadcasters is viewers for commercials. In order to turn those individual viewers into a packaged, uniform commodity that can be served up to potential purchasers—that is, advertisers—broadcasters have turned to the ratings services, which attempt to measure total numbers of viewers for any program according to various criteria, including age and income level. Ratings provide the "empirical evidence" that broadcasters need if they are to demonstrate to advertisers that their money is well spent.

Whether the ratings numbers are accurate in terms of volume (and this is often disputed) is of less importance to the industry than whether they are collected fairly and impartially. This is because ratings are a kind of currency, like paper money, and currencies only work if everyone agrees on their underlying value. The currency of ratings allows a broadcaster to say to an advertiser, for instance, "I will deliver an audience of 450,000 at 6 p.m. each weekday in return for our rate card fee of so much per thousand viewers." Another broadcaster might then undercut that offer by serving up higher audience numbers, or a lower cost per thousand, or both. This is competition at work, with ratings providing the numerical data necessary to making rational choices.

Implicit in the sales pitch for audiences-as-product is the promise that they are composed of happy campers; no sponsor wants to purchase a disgruntled audience. This guarantee is provided by the commercial television industry's oddly illogical, but universally accepted formula for audience satisfaction. Why do audiences watch programs? Because they like them. How do we know they like them? Because they watch them. On this tissue of sophistry rests the prime axiom of commercial broadcasting: "Give the audience what it wants." Even more perniciously, this axiom is extended into the realm of quality: Why do audiences watch our programs? Because they're good. How do we know they're good? Because audiences watch them.

In the real world of network television, on the list of variables that actually determine a program's audience ratings, quality often ranks relatively low. It may be less significant than such key determinants as the program's place in the broadcast schedule, the popularity of its lead-in and lead-out programs, what's on competing channels, marketing expenditure, and so on. It is part of the logic of commercial broadcasting that this is as it should be, and that any attempt to make objective, normative judgments about program quality in broadcasting is bound to be authoritarian and oppressive, or at least ill-advised and counterproductive—an unwarranted interference with the transcendent moral authority of the free market. It is part of the logic of commercial broadcasting that audiences should, and do, make judgments of quality for themselves, through their choices in the free, self-disciplining market. It is an ironclad principle celebrated as consumer sovereignty.

The consumer sovereignty approach to quality (which presumes that the competitive market will sort it out) finds favour among industry executives because it lets them avoid difficult moral and aesthetic issues that cluster around the idea of actual, normative, quality. And that's a relief for them, because engaging honestly with quality might well result in program expenditures not directly related to audience size and advertising income. In other words, wasted money and lower profits.

It is a fundamental tenet of capitalism that competitive markets contrive to produce products of the highest attainable quality at the lowest feasible price. The basic or idealized explanation for this is that an entrepreneur who offers a product or service that proves to be inferior to, or more expensive than, one offered by a competitor down the street will lose business to that competitor. Consumer sovereignty rules, and consumers (who are assumed to be rational) will choose the better value. This in turn is a powerful incentive for the uncompetitive business to improve its product or lower its price, or both, if it wants to survive. In this way, overall product quality ratchets up, as price trends downward. We see this at work every day in markets like clothing or consumer electronics, where a tangible product is being manufactured and sold. In competitive markets, all things being equal, the good drives out the bad.

But when this logic is applied to the commercial media market, the market that produces television programs and uses them to assemble audiences to sell to advertisers, it breaks down. A paradox arises. In the highly competitive television market, even though consumer sovereignty is well served, economic success may well be an indicator of lower, and not higher, quality in programming. Product quality will indeed rise over time thanks to market dynamics—but the product in question, the commodity being bought and sold, is audiences. What is a high-quality audience-product in the eyes of the advertisers, its potential purchasers and consumers? The high quality audience has three characteristics: the correct demographics; the largest numbers; and the lowest price. Dramas, sitcoms, newscasts, and reality shows are what broadcasters offer up to pull together the audiences desired by advertisers; the less money they spend in that process—in program production—the better for both broadcaster and advertiser. And so, in a competitive market, the investment made by broadcasters to assemble a given audience will be forced inexorably downward. And because there is an obvious, direct relationship between the cost of programs and their quality (again, all other things being equal), program quality will necessarily follow the same downward trend.

This happens not because of some flaw in human nature in general, or in the character of media managers in particular (though these may exist). The question, asked by many a media scholar, of whether, left to its own designs, popular culture gravitates towards the laudable or the dire, is the wrong question when it comes to commercially sponsored media. What happens to quality in commercial media happens precisely because popular culture is not left to its own designs. What happens is the result of the mechanical operations of the market, combined with the supremely rational behaviour of large corporations. Whatever they might once have been, by the late twentieth century large corporations had come to see their sacred responsibility as maximizing the value of the assets under their control, on behalf of corporate shareholders. The quality of programming is in principle irrelevant to this goal, so long as it is within legal and regulatory bounds, and therefore will not expose the corporation to legal penalties. As CBS programming executive Arnold Becker asserted, "I'm not interested in culture. I'm not interested in pro-social values. I have only one interest. That's whether people watch the program. That's my definition of good, that's my definition of bad."[74]

So economic success for commercial broadcasters operating in a competitive market implies, as a necessary corollary, mediocre programming. This is Gresham's Law of commercial media: where media are supported by advertising in a competitive market, the bad drives out the good.[75]

The evidence: critics express their astonishment on the rare occasions when an anomaly occurs in the form of a great program on a commercial network. These exceptions prove the rule, as do genuinely high-quality television programs routinely turned out by broadcasters and producers that do not rely on commercial sponsorship, such as subscriber-supported HBO and Netflix. Subscriber-financed broadcasters and producers operate in a market in which programs (and not audiences) are the product being sold, and to the extent that classic market dynamics affect them, they tend to force program quality upward, rather than down. As they compete for new customers, these networks take risks, pushing the envelope of existing program formats in order to build on their existing subscriber base. (Public broadcasters, for their part, ought to operate entirely outside that market, adhering to standards that are determined according to public service rather than, or in addition to, popularity.)

When *The Guardian* newspaper asked its arts and television reviewers to pick all-time best TV dramas, the list, which was topped by *The Sopranos*, was overwhelmingly composed of public broadcasting productions (mainly BBC) and American subscription channel productions, mostly HBO.[76] While subscription channels do rely on audience popularity (as expressed in subscriber revenue) for their survival, they have much more freedom to experiment, and to serve niche audiences, than do commercial broadcasters. The same applies to the new breed of Internet-delivered services, like Netflix. Their original programming is designed to appeal to existing and potential subscribers—actual viewers—rather than to advertisers, and thus the worst of the dynamics of Gresham's Law are avoided. Program budgets are shaped by a desire to expand subscription numbers, rather than to supply low-cost solutions for advertisers. Expanding subscription numbers will frequently require pushing boundaries and taking risks—exactly what risk-averse commercial broadcasters and their advertiser clients try to avoid.

Nevertheless, subscription-based services must still rank their successes according to popularity, as registered in subscriber levels. There is more flexibility in this arrangement, and more scope to allow struggling shows to grow and improve, or to find an audience over time. But in the end it is popularity and profit, and not public service, which determines what gets aired.

ADVERTISING'S INSIDIOUS IMPACT

It might be asked whether advertising per se, removed from any context of competitive market dynamics, is a corrupting influence on programming. In other words, might it be possible for a public broadcasting system like the CBC to accept advertising and still maintain the highest standards of program quality, as defined within the context of a public-service mandate? After all, it's the competitive pressure to produce audiences at lower and lower cost that drives quality down in the purely commercial market. If that dynamic could be removed, would it not be possible to maintain program standards and still benefit from advertising revenue? Recent senior CBC managers have answered in the affirmative; their predecessors were not so sure.

A compelling account of the real-world impact of advertising on CBC Television has been provided by one of Canadian public-service broadcasting's founders and one of its most reliable historians, W. Austin Weir. Writing in 1964, he notes that an increasingly heavy reliance on commercial sponsorship on both CBC radio and television had led to "a subtle change in the approach of both administrative and production staffs to commercial programs. The saleability of programs now became a prime consideration and the thinking of program staff consciously or unconsciously, but inevitably, was directed very largely to the production of saleable programs." The impact was worse on television than it was on radio. "In radio up to the [1950s], commercial programs were produced mainly ... by sponsors through their agencies. The CBC Commercial Department, in addition to being a sales and service organization, was also a buffer between sponsors or their agencies and the CBC Program Department." But television was so much more expensive than radio that most agencies dropped out of the production business, and programs were produced mostly in-house by the broadcaster. At CBC, "the Commercial Department was merged with the Program department as a sales division and ... [p]rogram executives assumed direct responsibility for meeting the steadily expanding monthly sales targets. Program producers became directly exposed to the demands and pressures of agencies and sponsors."

Weir said he had observed "a major slide toward commercialism" in CBC Television: "More and more the thinking has had to be what will please sponsors, what will get maximum audiences, what will sell .... *Commercial pressures are natural, persistent, inexorable, and those who have never been in the business have no idea how insidious and compelling they can be in the face of tightening budgets.*"[77] (Emphasis added.)

While there is a theoretical argument to be made that public service successfully could coexist with commercial sponsorship, on-the-ground realities militate powerfully against it, as Weir's first-hand account testifies. The logic of neo-liberalism shows no sign of losing its grip on politics, and within that logic, the public broadcaster that relies on advertising revenue finds itself on a slippery slope that will lead, over time, to lower public subsidies (always a desirable outcome from the neo-liberal perspective) and therefore to yet greater need for commercial sponsorship (also desirable, because it reduces the requirement for public subsidy while at the same time serving business interests).[78]

Moreover, from the point of view of modern management culture, efficient administration of any hybrid public-service/commercial broadcasting system such as the CBC demands that advertising revenues be maximized. Allowing potential revenue to go uncollected is the very definition of management irresponsibility. It's also an enormous political liability when it comes time to negotiate public subsidies.[79] While the culture of public-service broadcasting ought to be completely different from the culture of for-profit commercial broadcasting, as a practical matter the intrusion of the advertising economy makes that distinction difficult to achieve and maintain. As does the pervasive neo-liberal assumption that the administrative methods of private industry are always superior to those of public-service enterprises.

Not all arguments against advertising in broadcast media are political or economic. Advertising intrudes into content in ways both overt and subtle. In the first case, as already noted, advertisers typically do not want their products to be associated with controversial programming or programming of a serious nature in which commercial breaks are an obvious and annoying distraction; thus, many a brilliant program idea is smothered before ever seeing the light of day. But the very presence of advertising breaks in a program schedule shapes the structure and content of the programs themselves. In contrasting the programming of Britain's hybrid commercial/public-service ITV network with that of BBC television, media scholar and television producer Richard Rudin notes that the public broadcaster's advertising-free schedule was able to adapt a program's length to the requirements of its content (for example, talk shows could be extended by five or ten minutes if necessary to adequately explore an idea, or a drama might need an extra five minutes to complete a satisfying narrative arc). But commercial broadcasters, "have to be virtually obsessive in keeping to the times scheduled and paid for by advertisers. These breaks are now computer-controlled, and live output such as rolling news channels have to structure their output round the advertising breaks …. An ITV comedy, soap opera or drama not only had to fit a commercial half-hour (usually about 26 minutes of actual programme time) but had to have a narrative 'hook' to keep the audience through the mid-way commercial break."[80]

There is indeed a Gresham's Law operating in commercially sponsored television—the bad does drive out the good—but the dynamic is fuelled not by any implicit preference among the "masses" for junk; it is a feature of the dynamics of the commercial media market in which producers compete for advertisers by selling audiences. Richard Stursberg misunderstands this when he writes in his memoir that, under his administration and its new, populist programming strategy, "There would be only one measure of success: audiences. If Canadians did not watch, it meant they did not care .... In the words of the BBC, whose slogans are plastered all over the walls of White City, their great studio complex in west London, 'Audiences mean everything to us'."[81]

Of course, what is meant by this slogan is not 'ratings mean everything to us'. It means, in fact, exactly the opposite: Service to our audiences is what we are all about.

CHAPTER 6

DEFINING QUALITY IN PUBLIC BROADCASTING

Commercial broadcasting and public-service broadcasting are essentially two different industries, producing two different products, according to two different business plans. Public broadcasting produces programming that is intended to inform, enlighten, and entertain a citizenry. Commercial broadcasting, on the other hand, produces audiences, which are sold to advertisers, in the interests of corporate shareholders' return on investment; its programming is a secondary product, used to assemble marketable audiences. Put another way, public media uses public money to make programs in the public interest; commercial media use programs to make money for shareholders.

Audience ratings services exist solely as an adjunct to the commercial media industry, so that the commodity being produced—audiences—can be quantified according to a uniform metric. This is why ratings are an inappropriate way to measure the quality of any given program. Ratings are intended to measure only one aspect of a program—its ability to assemble an audience. The quality, or normative merit, of the program being used as bait is another, essentially unrelated, issue, and must be decided on different grounds.

If ratings tell us next to nothing about the quality of a radio or television program, what does? How is it that critics like the *Globe*'s Doyle and his colleagues can claim to know quality when they see it, and criticize CBC Television for not producing enough of it? What did Lord Reith have in mind when he spoke of bringing only the "best" to the BBC's audiences? What are we talking about when we talk about quality in media production?

In his memoir, Richard Stursberg explains that, before he instituted his ratings-grabbing populist program strategy at CBC Television, "there were no objective performance standards" in place at the corporation. Success was measured not by ratings, but in terms of what Stursberg dismisses as "vague notions" of public service and distinctiveness. Prior to his arrival, he writes, people at the CBC presumed that if a program was popular, on their own network or a competitor's, "it must be vulgar and stupid." But, he insists, the "most popular American shows that Canadians watched in their millions were not poorly made rubbish. To the contrary, they were often beautifully realized, well written, well acted, well directed and well produced. The top shows—*Law & Order*,

CSI, Desperate Housewives—were exceptionally good by any standards."[82]

Well, surely not *any* standards: Stursberg's definition apparently speaks to quality in terms of the craftsmanship involved in making these shows—the production values. The shows he cites are well-written, acted, directed, and produced examples of the craft of television-making. But artifice is only one dimension of quality. To use an obvious example, the film director Leni Riefenstahl's 1935 paean to Nazism, *Triumph of the Will*, has been widely recognized as a technical triumph—beautifully shot, produced, edited, and so on—but utterly meretricious. Some critics would argue more recent hit programs like *Breaking Bad* and *True Detective* share that distinction.

In order for a program to be characterized as good in the normative sense of that word, it clearly must have more going for it than technical excellence. This is particularly true in the context of public-service broadcasting, which sets its sights higher than simply amusing or entertaining its audience. Exceptionally good public-service programming aims to be the best it can be technically. But it must also contribute to what might be called the moral economy of the nation. It should in some way, large or small, leave viewers better than they were. Better, more informed and involved citizens; better, more fulfilled human beings. We may well ask whether Stursberg's benchmarks—*Law & Order, CSI,* and *Desperate Housewives*—are "exceptionally good" in this sense.

In their desperate attempt to achieve a ratings turn-around at CBC Television, Stursberg and his programmers poured the network's dwindling resources into making television shows that drew audience ratings that were occasionally comparable to the mostly American content on the private networks. The programs, from police procedurals to reality shows (the CBC euphemistically calls the latter "factual entertainment"), are virtually indistinguishable from their American phenotypes in every respect except setting. The question this strategy was supposed to answer was one asked by both the ill-informed and the wilfully perverse among the public broadcaster's critics: "How can you justify spending all those millions of taxpayer dollars if your ratings are so dismal?"

In other words, in responding to the jibe about inferior ratings, the CBC accepted the logic on which it is based. But the logic of the equation, quality equals high ratings, is false, from a number of points of view.

- Audiences are able to select their viewing choices only from the menu that is placed before them by broadcasters in their broadcast schedules. What's offered in the schedule is determined, in the case of advertising-supported broadcasters, by advertisers, not audiences. To the extent, then, that audiences are able to "vote" for their preferences by watching, they are picking and choosing among an artificially (and arbitrarily) restricted selection. What they would really prefer to be watching might well be none of the above.

- The level of consumption of a product says nothing about its quality, about whether it's good or bad. It speaks rather to such considerations as price, availability, the absence of options, marketing cleverness, and any number of cultural considerations such as fads and peer pressure. Just as quality is not always rewarded by popularity, popularity is not always a sign of quality.

- Even conceding, for the sake of argument, that high ratings can be a reliable indicator of genuine popular demand for a program or genre of programming, it still does not follow that high ratings equals high quality. It is possible, even routine, for people to sometimes desire what's not desirable—not a worthy object of desire, or more concisely, not good. And this can mean not good for the individual in question, or not good socially, or not good in a more abstract, normative sense, or all three.

So we're back to the original question: what are we talking about when we talk about quality in television programming? If the goal of public broadcasting is to provide quality content, how do we measure success or failure? If not ratings, then what?

The puzzle has received some attention from communications scholars in recent years. The hope is that some guidelines can be developed that will allow a broad consensus to be formed around quality judgments. One approach to defining quality is to turn for answers to the people who produce television for a living, the artists and artisans who make a profession of television programming of all kinds. Research into professional attitudes to determining quality, gleaned through dozens of interviews and summarized by media scholar Irene Costera Meijer, boils the issue down to the following checklist:

- Were the craft skills that went into the making of the program of a high standard?
- Was the program adequately resourced?
- Was it serious and truthful?
- Was it relevant to the concerns of the day?
- Did the storytelling touch the emotions?
- Did it appeal to curiosity/provoke thought?
- Did the program-maker have a clear objective? And push to achieve it?
- Did the program-maker have a passion/ commitment that gave energy to the program?
- Was the program innovative, original, or adventurous?
- How did the audience react to it—in appreciation as well as numbers?[83]

What is noteworthy about the criteria suggested by these media professionals is that they say almost nothing about audience size. Only the last of the questions above implies that ratings may, at some level, be a necessary— though not sufficient—indicator of quality.

Another way academics have approached the problem

is to break the concept into categories: sender-use quality; receiver-use quality; craft (or professional) quality; and descriptive (or truth) quality.

Sender-use quality is judged according to how well programming fulfills the needs and desires of the broadcaster. In the case of a commercial broadcaster, that will boil down to how much money the program makes. It's not quite so simple in the case of a public broadcaster like the CBC, where determining quality will involve such criteria as conformity to the broadcaster's official mandate and more generally to a responsibility to inform, educate, and entertain a national audience.

Receiver-use quality is quality in the eye of the beholder: as a subjective measurement it can be and often is completely idiosyncratic. One viewer's hockey bliss is another's outrage at violence on ice; even the most brilliant documentaries seldom have broad appeal, but are intensely enjoyed by self-selecting audiences. Moreover, audiences of different cultural backgrounds may respond differently to the same program, taking away different meanings.

Craft quality is what gets rewarded by prizes refereed by industry practitioners. It is the expression of the hard-won skills of the media professionals who make up the cast and crew of any production. It is the quality that, along with talent and inspiration, makes a screenplay or a musical performance great.

The fourth category, descriptive quality, is the classification most likely to cause serious debate. The question that has to be answered is: how close does this program come to portraying the world in as it really is? Does the program, whatever its genre, make an honest, sincere, and responsible attempt to present the truth about life? For commercial purposes, this may not matter. For a public-service broadcaster, however, the issue is of paramount importance, even in the context of entertainment programs.

Broken down in this way, the task of measuring quality in programming becomes less daunting, and entirely removed from the brutal, reductionist realm of ratings. It's possible to imagine a continuing conversation between programmers and the public that could arrive at a kind of evolving consensus. It becomes possible to answer the question, if not ratings, then what?

CHAPTER 7

PUBLIC BROADCASTING AND THE NEWS

Freedom of the press is a central pillar of any democracy for the simple reason that citizens must have access to news and information to make informed decisions. They also need access to a broad spectrum of opinion and analysis on matters of public importance. It is the job of journalists to provide that information and interpretation, which today is transmitted to us in a bewildering number of vehicles, which we refer to collectively as the news media. For most Canadians it's an obvious truth that the production of news and current affairs programming is the single most important responsibility of their public broadcaster. Most Americans, on the other hand, believe that news ought to be provided through the private broadcasting market, although a glance at the low esteem in which Americans hold their news services (see below) would seem to indicate a colossal failure of the market to produce what's needed.

But even in Canada, the notion that news coverage is a key role for public broadcasting was highly controversial when radio was young; newspapers considered the news to be their exclusive bailiwick and strenuously objected to the competition. The CBC did not begin broadcasting news on its national radio network until 1934, when Charles Jennings, the father of long-time ABC anchor Peter Jennings, read a script prepared for him by the Canadian Press, the Canadian newspapers' co-op news agency. The CP would continue to supply CBC's news until 1941, when wartime exigencies gave the public broadcaster the opportunity to set up its own news service, with regional correspondents across Canada and reporters covering the battlefields of Europe.

Although the work of individual reporters such as Peter Stursberg, Matthew Halton, Marcel Ouimet and Bob Bowman is justly celebrated, the CBC news organization was, in wartime, anything but the independent service that is strives to be today. It frequently operated as an arm of government, and a propaganda tool—though not without strenuous resistance from the small corps of journalists who did their best to follow professional injunctions of independence and objectivity.[84] Following the war many private radio stations built modest newsrooms covering local crime and politics, and when private television dawned, news was part of the network schedule. Without wishing to denigrate the efforts of individual journalists involved, it is fair to say that a minimum of expense and commitment went into private network TV news. And in the absence of CBC's subsidized operations and the standards they set, it would have been even worse. Covering the news nationally, let alone worldwide, was an expensive undertaking and private broadcasters were unable and unwilling to do the job. That remains the case today, with the nation's television news organizations operating for all intents and purposes on skeleton crews, relying heavily on foreign news agencies for overseas coverage, and withdrawing from domestic regional bureaus so that spending on domestic news is reduced to the bare minimum assumed to be tolerable by audiences, advertisers, and the CRTC. The CRTC takes a hands-off approach when it comes to news operations of the stations it regulates: "The Commission believes that ... there are sufficient market incentives to ensure that audiences will continue to receive a variety of local news without regulatory requirements. News programming is a key element in establishing a station's identity and loyalty with viewers and it is generally profitable."[85] In radio, this policy has resulted in the virtual extinction of original news reporting, and dramatic reductions in scheduled newscasts. Only CBC provides a comprehensive radio news service, and it, too, has lost much of its resource base in a recent cost-saving merger with CBC Television news.

The facts point to a different conclusion than the CRTC's. A large part of the problem lies in the progressive concentration of ownership in the hands of a very few media conglomerates, the related trend to vertical integration as a profit-maximizing measure, and the steep costs of debt associated with industry mergers and acquisitions. It all started with the newspaper industry.

THE DRIFT AWAY FROM DIVERSITY

The growth of newspaper chains in Canada and the consequent decline in the numbers of independent publishers has long been identified as a threat to diversity of opinion, and with good reason. In 1915 there were 138 daily newspapers in the country owned by 135 publishers, for an independent ownership share of nearly one hundred percent. By 1953 the growth of newspaper chains had become significant; the number of dailies had dropped to eighty-one, owned by fifty-seven publishers, for an independent ownership share of about sixty-six percent. By 1990 the total number of dailies was holding steady, but the share of the industry held by independent publishers had plummeted to seventeen percent. By 2015 it was just one percent; four big chains owned the rest—Postmedia, Torstar, Power Corp., and Transcontinental.

For a time it had been possible to argue that the newspaper chains were able to offer better salaries and working conditions for journalists, and therefore more professional, high-quality news coverage. But by the first decade of the twenty-first century, that was clearly no longer the case: mergers and acquisitions had left the handful of corporate owners left standing heavily burdened with debt, which they serviced mainly by reducing personnel costs. The numbers of newspaper journalists in the nation plummeted in wave after wave of layoffs. Significantly, the numbers of reporters employed by local newspapers in the Parliamentary Press Galley in Ottawa and in the provincial legislature equivalents plunged, as publishers replaced them with the chains' own syndicated coverage. Beat reporters, who specialized in topics such as education, labour, technology, science, medicine, and the environment, were replaced by less expensive, more productive general assignment reporters. (However, the number of working journalists in all media in Canada has remained relatively stable over the past decade: see below.)

Nearly half a century ago a special Senate Committee on Mass Media (the Davey Committee) expressed alarm that "the control of media is passing into fewer and fewer hands, and ... experts agree that this trend is likely to continue and perhaps accelerate." The committee concluded that "this country should no longer tolerate a situation where the public interest in so vital a field as information [is] dependent on the greed or good will of an extremely privileged group of businessmen." And it recommended that a Press Ownership Review Board be established to approve or reject mergers between, or acquisitions of, newspapers and periodicals. It was to use one basic guideline: "*All* transactions that increase concentration of ownership in the mass media are undesirable and contrary to the public interest unless shown to be otherwise." (Emphasis in original.) A decade later, the Kent Commission on newspapers came to similar conclusions.

In 2006 the Senate Standing Committee on Transport and Communications released a report on its three-year study, which warned that the then-current levels of concentration of media ownership posed a threat to news diversity and quality, and criticized the CRTC and the Competition Bureau for their ineffectiveness in dealing with the problem. The report lamented the lack of funding for the CBC and its news operations, and detailed worsening employment conditions for working journalists in both newspapers and electronic media.

Because newspaper reporters supply the lion's share of original reporting both nationally and locally—stories that are eagerly read in television newsrooms by editors who then assign them to be "scalped" by camera crews and TV reporters—when print newsrooms shrink, the entire news ecology suffers. A healthy newspaper industry supplies a rich diet of news fodder to the television newsrooms of the nation, raising issues and revealing facts that those newsrooms ignore at serious risk to their own credibility.

When television news blossomed in the decade following World War II it not only transformed people's news consumption habits, it also transformed the product. For most network newscasts, the complete menu of national and international news had to be distilled into about twenty-two minutes, with a heavy emphasis on pictures. Because of a television newscast's linearity, whatever story was selected to lead the program was given enormous emphasis as the most important event of the day, whether or not the attention was warranted; a newspaper that day might have had half a dozen or more stories on its front page, plus an index of coverage to be found inside. The evening newscast on network television was typically supplemented by a weekly hour of current affairs documentaries and interviews, which, depending on the network, skewed more or less toward infotainment. The medium made necessary the invention of the chief presenter, or anchor, whose personality and delivery style inevitably affected viewers' response to news stories. This was gatekeeping par excellence: never before, perhaps, had news been so tightly managed as in the era of the network TV newscast's so-called golden age, roughly from the 1950s to the 1990s.

Yet, for all its limitations, television was undoubtedly the most powerful news medium yet invented, bringing stories to viewers in their living rooms with unprecedented immediacy and realism. The real question is, to what extent did television news, in its half-century of hegemony, succeed in fulfilling its social responsibility to inform the public. Apparently, not well at all: despite dramatic increases in the general level of education and an increase in access to information through television news, Americans in the 1980s showed no improvement in general levels of political knowledge over their parents in the 1940s. At the same time there was a sharp decline in almost all forms of political participation.[86] Television news was not to blame, but it clearly was not a panacea.

The veteran NBC news producer Reuven Frank

pointed out many years ago that television news operates at a disadvantage to the newspaper when it comes to providing a balanced menu of information to its audience:

> A newspaper … can easily afford to print an item of conceivable interest to only a small percentage of its readers. A television news program must be put together with the assumption that each item will be of some interest to everyone that watches. Every time a newspaper includes a feature which will attract a specialized group, it can assume it is adding at least a bit to its circulation. To the degree a television news program includes an item of this sort … it must assume its audience will diminish.[87]

Current studies strongly indicate that for the foreseeable future conventional radio and television will remain our principal sources of news, though delivery platforms and receiving devices will undoubtedly change. Revolutions in the technologies of transmission and reception of news and information do not alter or diminish the need for timely, accurate, and reliable news prepared and delivered by professionals in accordance with professional standards of fairness and integrity. Nor do they change the essential nature of the information that needs to be shared: information about government, its administration, and the democratic process, about world affairs, about health and security, about coping with the complexities of everyday life.

TV NEWS AS PUBLIC SERVICE

Television news still matters. Despite encroachments from the Internet, it remains an important, often the most important, source of news for Canadians. We watch more, not less, television news each year, and we rank it far above Internet news sources such as blogs and social media in terms of reliability.[88] We count on it.

The operations of Gresham's Law—the bad drives out the good—and its impact on commercial TV programming have already been described. This dynamic is of particular concern in terms of television's role in establishing and maintaining democratic values and the marketplace of ideas, where it inevitably leads to a relentless downward pressure on costs associated with programming of news and documentaries. Market pressures militate against both the allocation of air time devoted to maintaining public space in media, and the quality of content appearing in that space. Free market dynamics, far from serving the public interest in a lively public space, conspire against that interest. It is a public good, and therefore, by definition, unprofitable. Evidence for the operation of this economic axiom, accumulated over three decades of deregulation in media markets, includes: eviscerated newsrooms; abandoned foreign bureaus; the industry-wide move toward infotainment; continuing concentration of ownership; and a continuing decline in public trust, which can be directly related to the decline in content quality.[89] In a world in which major media outlets are owned by a handful of mammoth corporations, the notion that profit might be sacrificed to public service is absurd. Modern business corporations are supremely rational entities and require that every aspect of their operations conform to the logic of profit.[90]

But corporations are also creatures of the state, and the state can regulate their behaviour. And where news is concerned, state regulation of broadcasters was a feature of the market in most industrialized nations throughout much of the twentieth century, until the rise of neo-liberal economic ideology in the 1980s and 1990s. In the United States, the swing to neo-liberalism and, with it, deregulation, roughly coincided with the purchase of the largest three broadcasters, ABC, NBC and CBS, by new corporate owners.[91] Deregulation meant the relaxation or elimination of statutory obligations that had required broadcasters to maintain professional news operations and present newscasts of prescribed length at prescribed intervals during the broadcast day. The ownership changes placed the major networks in the hands of corporate entities whose MBA-trained senior managers regarded news divisions as potential profit centres, and insisted that costs be reduced and revenues increased accordingly. The new entrepreneurial culture dictated that news programming be made more arresting and entertaining, so as to broaden its audience, making it more attractive to a wider array of advertisers.

The information quotient of news was progressively sacrificed to entertainment in the form of celebrity news, soft features, spectacle, and sensation. Physical appearance moved up the list of hiring considerations for on-camera personnel. The notion that one of the jobs of a responsible news organization was to present its audience with what it ought to know—even if it meant boring some of them some of the time, and even if it meant sometimes spending money on an investigative story that might not pan out—simply did not fit with the new business ethic. In the years following the takeover of CBS by financier Larry Tisch (1986) and then by Westinghouse (1995), to use a representative example, the number of CBS News foreign bureaus dropped from twenty-eight to four.

Since then, Gresham's Law has proved to be alive and well in commercially sponsored news operations across media platforms. The rationalization that swept through the industry bequeathed, not merely dumbed-down newscasts across the board, but the aggressively mendacious Fox News in the US and its tiny, abortive Canadian clone, the Sun News Network, not to mention a toxic cauldron of American talk-radio stations. In 2013, the time devoted to overseas news in American network newscasts was less than half what it had been in the late 1980s.[92]

Public confidence in television news has reflected this realignment of priorities over the past three decades. The Gallup organization's annual polling of the confidence Americans hold in various public institutions ranks TV news identically with "big business" and banks—just twenty-one percent of respondents saying they have "a great deal/quite a lot of confidence" in television news; thirty-eight percent have "very little or none." This puts TV news ahead only of private health insurance corporations (HMOs) at nineteen percent, and Congress, at thirteen percent. When Gallup started tracking confidence in American television news in 1993, confidence level was at forty-six percent; other evidence suggests it had been even higher a decade earlier.[93]

By contrast, in Europe and Canada, where public broadcasting continues to play an important, often dominant, role in the media mix, confidence in television news remains conspicuously higher than in the US. The data cannot be directly compared, but the differences in confidence levels are so dramatic that they do support the hypothesis that there is a link between the existence of prominent public broadcasting and the public's confidence in television news. Polling shows that public trust in television news throughout the European Union stands at sixty-one percent, a figure that is "a lot lower than it was just ten years ago."[94] Canadians are remarkably confident: a 2011 UBC/Angus Reid poll reported that ninety percent of respondents find television news to be "very reliable" or "reliable."[95] In other independent polling, CBC and CBC News Network are consistently ranked first by a wide margin as providing the best national news on television, with CTV and CTV News Channel second (although, paradoxically, CTV National News ratings are consistent chart-toppers); CTV leads the rankings for local news.[96]

As a hybrid, quasi-commercial operation, CBC Television news must constantly try to balance its public-service mandate with its role as a revenue generator for the network. This role, of course, demands that the news operation strive to maximize audience ratings. In its internal struggle with its conflicting demons, the commercial imperative is winning, and CBC Television news has slowly but inexorably edged in the direction of mass marketing and entertainment—in the direction of news as performance. Crime, weather, and sensation have been bumped up to the top of newscast lineups; serious documentaries have all but disappeared, to be replaced with panel discussions and YouTube video. Government is covered more and more as politics, as a spectator sport, and less and less in terms of public policy and its ramifications. Viewers are subjected to reporters gesticulating to camera as opposed to audio and video actuality; radio makes do with the TV audio track rather than items crafted specifically for that medium. There has been a noticeable decline in the calibre of reporting, writing, and editing, evidence of a waning commitment to (expensive) quality control.

CBC Television news has been drawn, over time, toward the commercial news model, both because it relies on commercial revenue, and because, like the rest of the Corporation, it has been forced to deal with serial cutbacks in funding and staff in recent decades. But it is also true that managers of the Stursberg era preferred the commercial news presentation style to public-service models like the BBC or PBS, which were perceived as stuffy. The result has been a deliberate attempt to raise the personal profiles of senior reporters and presenters, to afford them celebrity status. This may be a legitimate marketing ploy for commercial broadcasters who see themselves as trying to differentiate their otherwise generic product from the competition, but it is not appropriate to the values of public-service broadcasters. The simple reason is that where news is concerned, celebrity reporters and presenters inevitably impair the process of delivering information objectively, transparently, and without bias, real or apparent. The single most important prerequisite of a good journalist is humility. Reporters who wish to develop their personal brand should be steered elsewhere.

The personalizing of CBC News in the figure of the flagship television newscast's presenter Peter Mansbridge (grandiloquently called "chief correspondent") is a marketing technique filched from corporate branding, designed to humanize an otherwise faceless corporate entity. As such, it is expensive both in terms of salary and power relationships. The anchor, willy-nilly and regardless of intellectual acumen or journalistic skills, becomes the nine-hundred-pound gorilla in the newsroom because he or she is the franchise, the immediately identifiable corporate face of a lucrative enterprise. On his or her personal reputation rests the reputation of the entire news organization, as NBC discovered early in 2015 with Brian Williams (who embellished facts in his reports from war zones), and as CBS learned a decade earlier with Dan

Rather (whose *60 Minutes* story on George W. Bush's profligate Air National Guard career had to be retracted by the network 2004).[97] At CBC, controversy surrounding the lavish fees collected by Peter Mansbridge and "Senior Business Correspondent" Amanda Lang for speaking engagements with interest groups and corporations that frequently turn up in their newscasts can only have diminished the otherwise enviable reputation of the news division.[98] High-flying CBC News Network presenter Evan Solomon's flaming crash to earth in June 2015 is another sad example of the damage that can be done by this kind of scandal.[99] Solomon was fired after the *Toronto Star* revealed he had been introducing his contacts among the rich and powerful to an art dealer in return for commissions that amounted to hundreds of thousands of dollars. As is virtually universal practice in major news organizations, the CBC's journalistic policy guidelines expressly forbid employees from using their positions at the corporation for private benefit, so it was puzzling to many why Lang and Manbridge were not also disciplined, even though management, responding to press criticism, saw fit to change its policy and prohibit employees from accepting fees for speaking engagements in future.

FINDING A BALANCE

The question of how, and to what degree, the public broadcaster ought to compete with commercial networks in the area of news is controversial. Any journalist will tell you that the news is by its very nature a competitive business. Journalists are motivated by the scoop or beat; by being, as Edward R. Murrow's CBS News used to boast, "first with the best." The *Washington Post's* Watergate exclusives led *The New York Times* to devote expanded resources to an energetic effort to match the competition, and the result was good for the public. A similar, more recent, case could be made for the coverage of the robocall voter-suppression scandal and the Senate expenses scandals in this country, in which a variety of news outlets, including the CBC and Postmedia, challenged one another for the lead. This kind of competition is generally invisible to the casual observer, and its rewards are typically of the kind that only media professionals recognize and value. But competition within and between news organizations to be "first with the best" is healthy and productive of public good, and should be encouraged.

It is competition for ratings that winds up being so corrosive to standards and values. This is particularly true in markets like the United States, where public broadcasting and its values are an insignificant influence. In countries where public broadcasters are important players in the news environment, quality benchmarking can arrest the downward slide to the lowest common denominator in news programming. In Canada, this has been the case throughout much of the past half-century, but it will remain true only to the extent that the CBC news operation is adequately funded and (relatively) free of advertisings destructive impact. The trend, unfortunately, is in the opposite direction: in recent years advertising time in CBC news-casts has crept up while government funding has declined.

In considering the role of news in public-service broadcasting, it's important to think about the wider environment of news production and consumption. Within that ecosystem the public broadcaster has several special responsibilities:

- to provide a benchmark for quality—that is, to compete strongly in all aspects of news coverage, thus encouraging private broadcasters to be the best they can be;
- to offer the depth and context that private broadcasters find unprofitable to produce;
- to cover stories of high importance but low audience appeal, such as ceremonial events of national significance, political conventions, etc.;
- to provide a consistent, reliable, cumulative historical record for the nation, from all regions of the country and from significant foreign locations;
- to comment critically and reflexively on the overall health of the journalistic industry within which it operates; and
- to provide a competent, independent, and reliable source of emergency regional or nation-wide communication when needed.

If a public-service news operation does these jobs well, the role of ratings in judging its success—its value—fades in importance. The public broadcaster's responsibility is to the citizenry at large, and not to sponsors or corporate shareholders: audience numbers need to be considered in the broader context of the calibre of news available from all competing outlets within the system. If a public broadcaster can enhance the quality of commercially sponsored news on private networks by setting a high standard, it ought to do so, and consider that to be part of the public service it performs.

A NEW ERA FOR NEWS

In our current era of social media and blogs, anyone can deliver "the news." The distinction between traditional newscasters and the people formerly known as the audience is no longer as sharp as it once was. Social media have become an important source of shared news as delivered via "friends," a highly personalized editorial filter. Immediate audience feedback to traditional news outlets can shape coverage almost in real time, with listeners and viewers frequently playing roles as sources and fact-checkers. The news ecosystem is undergoing fundamental change, with television networks and newspapers competing for audiences online, their Websites providing similar mashups of text, audio and video content. Traditional print, TV, and radio news organizations continue to shrink, while new kinds of news providers are springing up: according to the Pew Research Centre, the top thirty of these new digital-only enterprises accounted for about 3,000 jobs in 2014, and were investing heavily in international reporting. *Vice Media* claimed thirty-five overseas bureaus; *Huffington Post* was operating in eleven countries; *BuzzFeed,* with news staff of 170 that included a Pulitzer Prize-winner, planned to expand to Mumbai, Mexico City, Berlin, and Tokyo. *Mashable* had a news staff of seventy and was able to entice a former *New York Times* assistant manager to become its chief content officer. Budgets, and audiences, however, remain relatively tiny as compared with the world's great traditional broadcast news organizations.

This drift toward digital, online platforms for news is of more than technical interest, because the medium shapes and massages the message. While television brought a new brevity to news delivery, the new online news media compress stories even further, and, just like conventional television, depend for their success on mass popularity, with all that implies for editorial priorities. Their chief advantages are their number and diversity, and their ability to link users to sources of related information with the touch of a finger. But whether anything more than a small minority of users will be willing or able to do their own research in this way remains to be seen.

The blessings of digital, online news media are mixed. Individual journalists have potentially greatly extended audience reach, because their work is available worldwide and is stored indefinitely in searchable databases; but unless they write for one of the "big brand" news operations, their reporting or commentary is likely to be lost in the sheer volume of material competing for audience interest. The Web does not limit the length of stories for lack of space, as do newspapers and conventional television newscasts. But studies show that it's difficult to persuade Web audiences to pay attention to longer items. Barriers to entry into the news publishing business are dramatically lower on the Web than in the bricks-and-mortar world, and it's easier to become a "journalist;" the necessary equipment is minimally expensive and research resources are vast. Though easy entry may well mean that professional standards are diluted or ignored, the Web also provides an automatic fact-checking facility via reader and viewer feedback, the ability to correct errors immediately, and endless space for opposing views.

As it currently exists, the online news industry consists of a great deal of aggregation and repurposing of other people's content, and very little original, investigative reporting. Few Web-based news operations can afford to pay more than a handful of editors, let alone general assignment reporters, beat specialists, or experienced foreign correspondents. As media analyst Bob Garfield wrote in *The Guardian*: "All that fantastic content [available on the Web] is paid for by venture capitalists making bad bets, established media companies digging into their savings accounts to pay the bills, displaced workers earning peanuts, amateurs, semi-pros, volunteers and monks."[100]

The increasingly ambitious migration online of the CBC has placed it in head-to-head competition with newspapers on the Web. This has raised objections from the Canadian newspaper industry to the effect that the public broadcaster is competing unfairly on the Internet because it receives a government subsidy. As Bob Cox, publisher of the *Winnipeg Free Press* and chair of the Canadian Newspaper Association, correctly points out, "the CBC was not set up to be a publicly subsidized media company. It was not set up to compete with newspapers that existed eighty years ago, or for that matter any media that have come along since that time that do not do over-the-air broadcasting." And yet, he complains, "it is now proposing to do just that—exactly the same thing *The Globe and Mail* or the *Winnipeg Free Press* is doing, only we do it without a public subsidy."[101]

It's an old complaint: as we saw earlier, the newspaper industry's grievance with public broadcasting goes all the way back to be beginnings of broadcast radio. When the BBC took to the airwaves in 1922 as the world's first national broadcaster, pressure from newspaper publishers resulted in a rule that prohibited it from presenting news bulletins until after the evening newspapers had hit the streets. In Canada, the CBC and its predecessor, the CRBC, were similarly hobbled in order to prevent "unfair" competition with newspapers. It was not until well into World War II that our public broadcaster was given the resources and mandate to mount a full-fledged news organization. Even then, though, almost all on-air commentary was outsourced to newspaper columnists and reporters.

The advent of digital, online media such as news blogs, aggregators and Websites have amplified the inter-media animosity. Newspapers, hit hard by declining ad revenue as sponsors migrate with readers to online media, have been trying to stay afloat by bulking up their Websites. The best of them have had real success both with ad revenue and with subscriptions. Britain's *Guardian*, for example, boasts nearly 25 million unique views (visitors) a month.

But broadcasters have so far proved to be more adept than newspapers at providing what audiences want when it comes to digital media on their laptops, tablets, and smartphones—grabby headlines, and concise, punchy, unambiguous prose accompanied by brief video clips, all organized in user-selected priorities. In the UK, the *Guardian* Website, for all its popularity, is a pale second to the BBC's in unique monthly views. In Canada, cbc.ca ranks twenty-second in the country's top 100 Web destinations, while the *Globe and Mail* and the *Toronto Star,* topping the newspapers, ranked forty-seventh and seventy-fifth, respectively.[102]

It is perhaps understandable, given the financial pressures facing the industry, that newspaper publishers would be angered and alarmed to see the CBC putting more of it resources into digital media. The Canadian Newspaper Association seems to think that digital media aimed at mobile devices is turf that rightly belongs to print media. In fact, whether the new digital media are a natural extension of print, or of radio and television, is a moot point. Sites like *thestar.com* and *cbc.ca* are an amalgam of both traditions. Broadcasters might as easily complain about newspaper Websites horning in on their territory, as vice-versa.

From a business point of view, most newspaper Web-sites closely resemble conventional television, in that they strive to achieve widespread popularity—high ratings—in order to sell advertising. On the other hand, the traditional paper-and-ink newspaper business plan closely resembles specialty television channels, in which substantial income is derived from subscriber fees, supplemented by ad revenue. In the special case of the CBC, the friction could be mitigated, if not completely resolved, if the public broadcaster were to forgo commercial sponsorship on all its platforms. Its current advertising revenue would then be available to commercial media, and the CBC would be free to a pursue public broadcasting agenda. That agenda ought to embrace the fundamental tenet of universal accessibility. To achieve that goal, it will be necessary to find a way to reduce or eliminate consumer data fees attached to downloads and streaming services. The most straightforward way to accomplish that is for BDUs to eliminate data charges on all digital content originating with the public broadcaster. If a quid pro quo is necessary, it can be found in the fact that the PSB will have relinquished the increasingly lucrative online advertising market to commercial enterprises, most of which are in the hands of these same BDUs.

The early twenty-first century may be the best of times for the news industry and for journalism, or the worst. It's too soon to tell. But as Ann Friedman wrote in the *Columbia Journalism Review*, we'd be well advised to behave as if it were the best, because the old model isn't coming back and news needs to adapt to that fact.[103] Once again, the role of a healthy public broadcaster is critical in this adaptive process. It can afford to take risks, and experiment. It is mandated to maintain benchmark standards in news gathering and production, and it understands the importance of doing so. It can provide a beacon of reliability and trustworthiness in a chaotic information landscape, sifting information from noise. But it needs to be properly financed.

CHAPTER 8

SUCCESS STORIES:
RADIO AND THE FRENCH LANGUAGE SERVICES

If the public broadcaster as a whole performed as well as either CBC Radio or the French-language radio and television networks operated under the umbrella of Société Radio-Canada, there would be no need for this book, or for ongoing debates about the relevance or necessity of the service. A 2015 Angus Reid poll found that eighty-eight percent of Quebecers (and ninety percent of francophones) hold "favourable" or "very favourable" views of their public broadcaster. Radio-Canada television enjoys a popularity on par with the best public broadcasters of Europe. The French service's successes reflect overall viewing preferences in Quebec, which are in sharp contrast with English Canada's: while anglophone Canadians spend more than three-quarters of their viewing time watching foreign (mostly American) programming,

French Canada splits its Canadian versus foreign viewing about sixty/forty in favour of the domestic product. Radio-Canada's television programming regularly draws an audience share of twenty percent in prime time, as compared with CBC Television at about eight percent in a good year.[104]

When, in late 2014, CBC/Radio-Canada President Hubert Lacroix announced plans to cut nearly twenty percent of the corporation's workforce over the succeeding five years, thousands of protestors took to the streets in Montreal, Sherbrooke, Trois-Rivières, Quebec City, Saguenay, Matane, Sept-Îles, Rimouski and Gaspé. Protest in the rest of Canada was confined to online comments and newspaper op-ed pages.

Indigenous French-Canadian programming on the CBC began with *Le Réveil rural* (The Farm Broadcast) in 1938, and the soap opera *Un Homme et son péché* (A Man and his Sin), which debuted the following year and ran for the next twenty-two years. A vibrant popular culture in all media has grown up around the root-stock provided in large measure by Radio-Canada radio and television. As cultural historians Mark Kasoff and Patrick James have observed, "In Quebec the state watches culture closely, and for good reason. A separate and thriving culture is the bellwether of French-Canadian *survivance*."[105]

Quebec journalist and professor Florian Sauvageau, writing in the journal *Mémoires vives* quotes a former colleague, the celebrated biochemist and science popularizer Fernand Séguin, on the significance of Radio-Canada to his province: "I remember two important events in our history: the arrival of Jacques Cartier ... and the arrival of Radio-Canada." The quip, Sauvageau continues, "nicely illustrates the importance of the role played by the CBC in the evolution of Quebec in the last century—first in radio and even more in television—in opening the world to Quebecers, in spreading their culture and in the construction of the 'Quebec identity'."[106]

Radio-Canada does not face a need to reclaim Canadian culture from American radio and television, as the English-language CBC services do. The ratings leaders in Quebec television are all locally produced, and so the major challenge for the French network is to differentiate its programming from that of TVA, its major commercial rival (owned by Quebecor). Radio-Canada's strategy has been to produce entertainment programming of cultural significance, and to dominate in news and current affairs. Instead of the populist *téléromans* on competing networks, Radio-Canada has focused on more expensive, quality series with high production values (*Les Hauts et les bas de Sophie Paquin*, *Tout sur moi*), and on edgier, unconventional sitcoms and sketch comedy shows. Documentaries and current-affairs programs like the enormously popular *Tout le monde en parle* and the investigative series *Enquête* are a regular feature of prime time; the fine arts are not unknown, as they are on the English network. Hockey vanished from the French network in 2004 when the regular Saturday night broadcasts of Montreal Canadiens games were relinquished to the private sports network RDS.

Superficially, the English television service could claim to have a similar schedule, and it was a source of frustration to former head of English-language programming Richard Stursberg that Radio-Canada television's audience share was twice that of its English counterpart. More than that, he resented the Board of Directors pointing to the French network as a model to be emulated. But there was, and is, an underlying, values-based distinction between the two. Stursberg set a course based on maximum audience ratings at virtually any cost, up to and including the airing of American game shows like *Jeopardy* and *Wheel of Fortune* to provide strong lead-ins to prime-time fare, programs which he insisted be tailored to attract the broadest possible audience. Can-con dramatic content, crafted by independent producers, was made with an eye to foreign sales, and therefore aimed at recognized genre stereotypes rather than regional or national authenticity. (At this writing the much-hyped *Schitt's Creek* was the best current example of this.) The foreign market available to Quebec productions is much smaller, and less tempting; programs are made with the domestic audience front-of-mind. Finally, NHL hockey was a cornerstone of the English schedule, providing nearly 400 hours of programming, bumping even the flagship newscast *The National* out of prime time during the long, long play-off season. Stursberg himself summed up the distinction that made such a difference in this bitter passage from his memoir:

The whole strategy is encapsulated in the broad claim that radio-Canada is about Culture and Democracy, culture here is meant to be taken with a capital C. Sylvain [Lafrance] would explain regally that it was about providing more demanding shows that strive to attain the highest possible standards. It was about setting the cultural and intellectual bar for French Canada.[107]

To find a success in English Canada in any way comparable to domestically produced programming in Quebec one has to look to radio, and specifically to CBC Radio One.

THE RADIO LANDSCAPE

The radio industry in Canada continues to surprise by its steady growth: between 2000 and 2014 revenues increased from $1.07 billion to $1.6 billion, an all-time high. Profit margins were over twenty percent, more than double the average for all industries. (It's a trend occurring worldwide.)[108] At the same time, corporate mergers in the industry were putting ownership of stations in fewer and fewer hands, and the mood in government in Ottawa continued to favour minimal regulation. There remains, however, some real diversity on the Canadian airwaves, and the country is preserved from playlists identical to those on American stations thanks mainly to the

CRTC's Canadian content regulations. Can-con quotas for radio began in the 1970s with a mandatory twenty-five percent Canadian-content rule, which has since risen progressively to forty percent in new licensing. Although commercial radio broadcasters initially complained loudly that Can-con regulations would doom their industry by driving away listeners, the opposite has happened. It is by now an accepted fact of Canadian cultural history that these regulations played a crucial role in the development of a vibrant Canadian music industry where none had existed before, and commercial radio continues to thrive as a beneficiary of that industry. Canada has become the second or third largest exporter of musical talent in the world.[109]

In 1975 CBC Radio eliminated commercial sponsorship and thus became for the first time an authentic public-service broadcaster, "free from vested interests." This extraordinary policy shift was proposed by CBC President Laurent Picard and implemented during the tenure of his successor, A. W. (Al) Johnson, a career public servant who held a Ph.D. in public administration from Harvard and had spent a decade as deputy provincial treasurer under Premier Tommy Douglas in the CCF-NDP government of Saskatchewan. Johnson's public-service instincts combined fortuitously with the reality of declining advertising revenue at CBC Radio (due largely to competition from the burgeoning television service) to allow him to take what seems today an impossibly radical step. At the time of the change, advertising was providing just sixteen percent of the radio service's total budget of $45 million. Johnson was also helped along politically by the commercial radio lobby in Ottawa, which had for decades been strident in its insistence that the public broadcaster was unfairly competing with commercial broadcasters for advertising revenue, reducing their profit margins.

Whether commercial and public-service media are truly in competition with one another is an interesting question. In one sense they are: if we consider audience numbers to be strictly limited, or "inelastic," as economists put it, then of course people watching public-service outlets cannot at the same time be watching commercial offerings. Commercial audience numbers will necessarily drop. But research suggests that audience numbers are in fact quite elastic. There is always a large pool of people who choose to watch or listen to nothing, because nothing on offer interests them. Public-service media draw at least some of their audience from that more discriminating pool, and to that extent have little or no impact on commercial media audience numbers. Backing that up, research in Europe has shown that boosting budgets for public-service broadcasting has no discernible impact on commercial broadcasting's audiences or revenues, and may in fact improve both through a "virtuous circle" effect as described in Chapter 4.[110]

In the years following the removal of advertising on CBC Radio, the service experienced a renaissance in programming that increased the already intense loyalty of an expanding audience and led it to leadership in its largest urban markets. The absence of advertising, serious attention to the arts and the world of ideas, top-quality, thoughtfully produced current affairs programming, and virtually one hundred percent Canadian content proved to be a winning formula. At the helm of radio during those years was a remarkable, BBC-trained producer named Margaret Lyons, who transformed the broadcast schedule with new and innovative national programs such as *As It Happens*, *Quirks and Quarks*, *The House*, *Sunday Edition*, and *This Country in the Morning*. Perhaps more significantly, she set about making the public broadcaster sound more like the people it served—more colloquial, more conversational, less stilted and officious. To that end she cultivated on-air talents that have since become iconic: Barbara Frum, Peter Gzowski, David Suzuki, Michael Enright, Vicki Gabereau, and many others.

A decade later, local and regional programming underwent a radical revision of its own, designed to ensure that programs in the morning and evening drives and lunchtime slots more closely reflected the diversity of the urban populations they served.[111] Serious and sustained effort was put into recruiting and training both on-air presenters and behind-the-scenes production staff from diverse ethnic and cultural backgrounds. These efforts were rewarded with solid ratings successes across the country. And the local success brought more and more listeners to the national programming: daily audience share for CBC Radio One in markets where there is a local station are uniformly double what they are in markets without a local presence. This experience could well be a model for revival of CBC's local and regional television.

CBC Radio is unique in its market: it has no competitors. Little on commercial radio bears comparison, either in terms of Canadian content, or in terms of intelligence, originality, and quality. CBC Radio currently accounts for about twenty percent of radio listening hours in Canada, an impressive figure given the number of options.[112] And audience loyalty is legendary: when a CBC listener turns on her radio and doesn't like what she hears, she doesn't go to another station; she turns her radio off. Regular CBC listeners spend an astonishing average of 400 hours a year with the radio services.[113] Sadly, it is an open question whether CBC Radio's reach will hold up now that the service has reduced original current-affairs programming, eliminated drama, and resorted to much more frequent repeats of its programming in the face of further budget cuts imposed both by Ottawa and by a management regime intent on finding ratings success in television, at all costs.

The elimination of radio drama as a cost-saving measure is particularly galling: it took place just as interest in radio podcasts was accelerating south of the border, where NPR expects to see declining over-the-air audiences more than replaced by podcast listeners. "Serial," produced in nine episodes for NPR by *This American Life* in 2014, was downloaded free from iTunes more than five million times for an average audience of more than 1.5 million listeners per episode. It may have been the medium's first breakout hit, but podcasting's popularity had been trending upward for some time, reaching nearly 40 million people in the US. It's possible that some variation of the podcast model will be the future of radio, though it's hard to see conventional over-the-air radio disappearing—particularly not public radio, which has public-service responsibilities, including universal access, to fulfill.

Some observers predict that half of all commercial radio stations will have vanished within a decade as music-seekers turn to streaming audio services like Spotify, Pandora, Songza, Deezer, and the many other services competing in this crowded market. It is estimated that half of all radio listening in Canada takes place in automobiles, but here too a shift to streaming audio is expected: car makers are equipping more and more new vehicles with Bluetooth, Internet, and satellite radio capabilities. CBC's entry into this field, music.cbc.ca, shows early promise as a showcase for Canadian talent, though for the moment it relies heavily on foreign content. But by their very nature, streaming music services fail to serve one of the most important objectives of public-service broadcasting, since they are in principle incapable of assembling a national audience for a shared experience. Nor do they provide the intelligent curation of conventional PSB stations employing announcers: on CBC Radio this feature has traditionally made listening a learning experience, and well-informed hosts have become valued companions to millions of listeners.

THE TRANSFORMATION AT RADIO 2

CBC launched a small, experimental FM network in 1948, on which it simulcast programming from the main AM network. Distinctive music and arts-oriented FM programming began in 1960, and in 1975 the network was renamed CBC Stereo. By 1997 virtually all of the original AM network had migrated to FM as well, and the branding identities were changed to Radio One and Radio 2. Until 2008 most of the music heard on Radio 2 was classical and jazz, and, like Radio One, the audience (on average significantly older than Radio One's) was fanatically loyal, though more modest in number. In that year, another Stursberg-backed initiative transformed the bulk of the Radio 2 schedule into what in commercial radio is known as an adult contemporary format, dramatically reducing classical-music content on weekdays to a little over four hours of predictable favourites during the midmorning. It was an overt attempt to boost the service's ratings by tapping into a younger demographic. "Radio 2's audience was aging," Stursberg had argued "If the senior service was not careful, it would lose the listenership of Radio 2 not to competitors, but to the grave."[114] This was a concern driven by advertisers' preference for younger demographics, ignoring the fact that the CBC's aging audience is undergoing a surge that will see it double in size as the baby boom generation turns sixty-five in coming years.[115] And younger audiences were in any case trending way from radio and onto streaming music services on the Internet. Stursberg's published view was that, ultimately, the classical music on Radio 2 "had nothing to do with Canadian culture."[116]

Listeners who had been accustomed to waking up to and driving home to symphonic music and jazz were now treated to a Canadianized version of the Top Forty. Fine music, but not their first choice, and anyway it was music they could hear elsewhere on the dial, or via the Internet on CBC Radio 3. At about the same time, the CBC announced it was shutting down the venerable CBC Radio Orchestra in Vancouver. There had once been five CBC orchestras; the others, in Winnipeg, Toronto, Montreal, Halifax, had been disbanded after earlier budget cuts in the 1980s. The Vancouver orchestra had for sixty-five years played an important role in Canadian classical music by commissioning, performing and recording new Canadian compositions. It had been the last of North America's radio symphonies, commercial networks having long since concluded that there was no profit to be made in maintaining such ensembles as Arturo Toscanini's NBC Radio Orchestra. In contrast, public broadcasters in Europe currently maintain a total of more than fifty radio orchestras: the BBC alone has five.

For Radio 2 aficionados, the changes were apocalyptic, and audience share collapsed. Columnist Jeffrey Simpson spoke for many when he wrote in *The Globe and Mail* that Radio 2 had been a "redoubtable" island of intelligence in an otherwise largely mindless broadcast environment. "Radio 2's distinguishing characteristic was its intelligence," he said. "It emphasized classical music because that kind of music was not easily available in private radio and because, throughout the ages, that form of music appealed to the intelligence and the deepest emotions of listeners … [It is] the deepest exploration of the human dilemma through music."[117] A House of Commons Committee chastised CBC managers for their folly, members of all parties expressing their dismay. The corporation defended the change by citing a need to attract a younger audience in order to remain "relevant," and by pointing out that there was a world of new Canadian contemporary rock music that was not getting airplay on commercial stations.

To mollify listeners, CBC introduced at the same time a clutch of audio channels on the corporate Website, which played continuous streams of classical, jazz, singer-songwriter and contemporary Canadian classical compositions. In his memoir, Stursberg explained the new service this way: "'You want classical music?' we would ask. 'Just go to the CBC Website and stream it on your sound system. There it will be. No commercials. No annoying commentary. Just classical music twenty-four hours a day.'" Those who felt this was a lame substitute for the intelligent presentation that had been the hallmark of Radio 2, Stursberg ridiculed as dimwitted fogeys.[118] That initial online content has since become a part of the broader music streaming service, cbc.music.ca.

Between 2000 and 2013 audience numbers for Radio 2 continued to shrink, though on-air personalities such as

Rich Terfry, Tom Powers, Tom Allen, and Laurie Brown were developing devoted followings comparable in their loyalty to those of earlier classical-music hosts like Eric Friessen and Jürgen Goth. (By contrast, audience share for the French-language equivalent, Ici musique, formerly known as Espace musique, which retained its jazz/classical format, more than doubled in the same period.[119]) Continual tweaking by talented producers has helped. It remains to be seen whether a weekday menu of classical warhorses surrounded by mainly Canadian adult alternative rock can satisfy audiences in the same way that programming dedicated exclusively to either format might.

Behind the remake of Radio 2 lies the same tacit, erroneous assumption that was made by Stursberg about television: that is, that the medium imposes strict constraints on the content. In the case of television, Stursberg insisted that only light, narrative entertainment and live events like sports were suitable and appropriate to the medium. In the case of radio, the assumption appears to have been that since private radio has become almost exclusively a purveyor of pop music in various genres and niches along with a smattering of talk-and-news stations, that lighter fare is the "appropriate" role for radio as a technology. Hence, for example, the tragic decisions to eliminate the radio drama department and the CBC Radio Orchestra. Again, what has actually determined the nature of content on private radio has been a calculus showing that what earns the most money is lowering costs and reliably serving up the kinds of audiences advertisers want.

There is absolutely no basis in logic or experience for the assumption that radio is no longer suitable for programming beyond the boundaries of pop music and news/talk formats. In fact, there is an excellent argument to be made for the continued exploration of the potential of radio and its emerging role in a world of broadband multimedia, podcasting, and streaming audio, listened to on all manner of portable digital devices.

A glance back at the history of CBC Radio provides some indication of the possibilities (though, of course, not a prescription for today). While music, mainly live and orchestral, was a mainstay of early radio—it filled time at reasonable cost and kept audiences entertained—between 1936 and 1941 the portion of the CBC broadcast schedule occupied by music fell from seventy to fifty-one percent. The reason? The CBC drama department had been formed in 1938, and during its first year producers read through more than a thousand submissions from aspiring playwrights, and broadcast 350 of them. Beginning with World War II, news and current affairs began taking over a larger portion of the broadcast day, but drama continued to be a mainstay. In 1941 the network produced a series of classic plays on themes related to the war against Fascism, starring some of the leading international stage actors of the time: Shaw's *St. Joan*; Ibsen's *An Enemy of the People*; Galsworthy's *Strife*; Drinkwater's *Abraham Lincoln*; Obler's *This Precious Freedom*, Shelley's *Hellas* and others. In the 1947 – 1948 season CBC Radio presented 300 plays, almost all of them works by Canadian playwrights. This does not include offerings from the flagship dramatic series *CBC Wednesday Night*, which broadcast classics from Shakespeare, Marlowe, Tolstoy, Shaw, O'Casey, and Eliot. These works were produced in studios in Vancouver, Halifax, Winnipeg, Montreal and Toronto, using Canadian producers and technicians and, for the most part, Canadian actors. As broadcast historian Austin Weir reported: "Canadian talent was being given genuine encouragement on an increasing scale, and—most important of all—there was a growing spirit of creative work being accomplished, which made the Corporation increasingly attractive to young and talented intellectuals."[120]

In addition, CBC Radio carried commercially sponsored Canadian variety, music, and drama, and a much larger offering of American commercial programming, including *Edgar Bergen and Charlie McCarthy*, *Our Miss Brooks*, *Fibber McGee and Molly*, *Ozzie and Harriet*, *Kraft Music Hall*, *The Aldrich Family*, and shows staring Bing Crosby, Jack Benny and Bob Hope.[121] The CBC farm broadcasts of the 1930s, 1940s, and 1950s engaged not only rural Canada but urban listeners as well, with their reality-based dramas about life among farm families and daily market reports. (The model was later exported to developing countries around the world.) Children's programming included iconic shows like *Maggie Muggins* and *Just Mary*.

RADIO'S FUTURE

The story of public service, creativity, and innovation on CBC Radio could be extended for many pages. The important point is that radio as a medium—whether over-the-air, live streaming, on packaged in podcasts—presents endless possibilities for audience engagement, entertainment, and education, and it does so at about a tenth of the cost of similar productions on television. Does television do it better? Sometimes, undoubtedly, but there is good reason to believe that children's programming, for instance, is sometimes better on radio, where the child's imagination is fully engaged, and where the kind of stultifying, hypnotizing effect produced by standard children's fare in video format is not an issue. For the same reasons, drama often works especially well on radio. Many sports fans prefer to listen to baseball or soccer on radio. Interviews of all kinds are frequently more intimate and revealing on radio than on television, just as comedy is often more creative and inventive. Why should it be assumed that well-produced and -acted, well-publicized radio drama is obsolete as a legitimate art form and vehicle of public service on radio? One of the last dramatic series produced by CBC Radio was *Afghanada*, a highly engaging and often moving series following the lives of Canadian soldiers fighting in Kandahar province. It ran for more than one hundred episodes over five years and drew an average audience ranging from 300,000 to 600,000 a week on radio and online. By any standard related to public service, this has to be considered a success. Current programs like *Wiretap*, *Spark*, *This Is That*, *The Debaters*, *DNTO*, *The Current*, *Vinyl Tap* and *The Signal*, along with perennial audience favourites like *Sunday Morning*, *Ideas* and *As It Happens* demonstrate that there is still plenty of scope for experimentation on radio. In our era of exploding technical possibilities in communication media, the CBC ought to be more fully engaged with radio than ever.

Which raises another issue. What many Canadians, CBC fans and foes alike, fail to consider is that serving the entire range of listener preferences, from pop and rock to classical, to jazz and world music to talks, documentaries and drama, comedy and variety, local, regional, national news and special events, on two over-the-air radio channels (in each official language), is simply impossible. In other words, it is not possible for CBC Radio to fulfill the demands of its public-service mandate with just Radio One and Radio 2 and their French-language equivalents. In Britain, BBC radio operates Radio 1 (pop/rock/urban); Radio 2 (adult pop/alternative); Radio 3 (classical, jazz, arts and drama); Radio 4 (the arts, ideas, current affairs); Radio 4 Extra (digital service/archival selections); and Radio 5 (live news and sports). In addition there are the associated individual Websites that support the over-the-air services, and which feature streaming audio, archives, and podcasts. There is no reason in principle why CBC Radio could not be expanded to more comprehensively serve its audiences on more frequencies, should Canadians demand it.

While CBC Radio's audience share is routinely three

times that of CBC Television, the corporation's management has chosen to deplete radio budgets to support the television services. Between 2009 and 2015, CBC Radio's budget was cut by more than $50 million, while CBC Television budgets went up. Over the same period, staff levels at CBC Radio were reduced by more than twenty percent while television staff cuts were just over three percent.[122] The results included reductions of fifty percent in local noon-hour programming, the shutting down of the legendary radio drama department, and much more frequent program repeats in the afternoon and evening. And in 2014 advertising reappeared on radio services for the first time since 1975, a giant step backward. In a split decision on CBC's application for permission to carry nine minutes of advertising an hour on Radio 2 and what was then called Espace Musique, the CRTC voted to allow advertising on a three-year trial, but only four minutes an hour. Commissioner Tom Pentefountas called the decision "crazy" pointing out that even if CBC's revenue expectations of $10 million a year were met (they fell far short, at $1.1 million), it was not worth alienating the loyal radio audience while diluting the services' distinctiveness for an increase in overall revenue of 0.06 percent.

The transfer of support away from radio, by a wide margin CBC's most popular services, to television was an unannounced policy decision that once again demonstrated how reliance on income from commercial sponsorship wrenches the focus of the public broadcaster away from public service and toward serving advertisers.

CHAPTER 9

THE PUBLIC BROADCASTER IN THE DIGITAL ERA

In the early days of the Internet and the Web, futurists wrote enthusiastically about the potential for anyone and everyone with access to a computer to become a publisher with a worldwide audience. There is truth in this vision, as the phenomenon of the viral YouTube video or monster ReTweet can attest. But as the Internet and its resources have expanded exponentially, the supply of the sought-after commodity of people's attention has necessarily dwindled relative to the demand. In a world in which there are (at this writing) well over two billion active Internet users, nearly three-quarters of whom are engaged with social media sites like Facebook, Google+, Instagram, and Pinterest; where there are well over 200 million tumblr and WordPress blogs, and about 220 million active Twitter accounts, it's not easy to be heard. Unless you're already famous: Katy Perry had 66 million

Twitter followers in 2015; Justin Bieber had 61 million and Barak Obama had 56 million.[123]

As a broadcast medium, the Internet can serve the same purpose as an over-the-air transmitter, moving programming from a production or storage centre to the audience (normally an individual, as opposed to a group). The difference is that, due to the very large storage capacity and the near-instantaneous accessibility in the digital environment, it is possible to support "on-demand" services via the Internet. Programming in virtually unlimited quantity can be warehoused on digital storage media so that audience members can retrieve it at their convenience, rather than having to wait for it to appear on a traditional broadcaster's scheduled transmissions. Where news is concerned, the Web makes it possible for individuals to create personalize newscasts, selecting stories from a menu of interest categories such as science, technology, politics, international affairs, and so on. The Internet is steadily gaining favour as a primary source for news, particularly among younger Canadians: more than half of eighteen to thirty-four-year olds now look to Internet sources, twice as many as turn to conventional television. TV remains the principal source for those over fifty-five. The thirty-five to fifty-four age group is about evenly split.[124]

The on-demand feature of Web-based media services is convenient, but it differs from traditional broadcasting in an important way. The veteran Canadian television producer Richard Nielsen has described the distinction eloquently:

Unlike the Internet, broadcasting is not about supplying a library to which the public has access. Broadcasting assembles a congregation. It is comparable to a concert hall or other meeting halls in our larger cities. Broadcasting is designed to provide a communal experience, an experience that helps build consensus by its very nature, a consensus that should impose the disciplines on [production] talent that ensure that its standards will be high enough to serve that function.[125]

Web-based services, for all their convenience, cannot for the foreseeable future replace public-service broadcasting as a tool for developing and enriching social solidarity. Personalized Web news services that assemble stories from a variety of sources can supplement, but are in no way a complete substitute for professionally produced national, regional, and local newscasts that keep listeners and viewers informed on a broad range of topics with stories that are, or ought to be, of interest to them as citizens of the nation and of the wider world. Broadcasting, with its power to vastly extend public space and facilitate dialogue, has well-proven potential to shape attitudes and values. And that is why, as Nielsen cautions, only "people who believe that such collective experiences foster creativity and advance human possibilities are willing to encourage it. Those who have other reasons for

mobilizing public opinion will see it as a danger and attempt to minimize its influence or, as in the US, channel it to achieve specific ends dedicated to religious or
political conversion rather than exploration."[126] Among
the most messianic proponents of the Web's potential for
social change are many staunch Silicon Valley libertar-
ians who view government as an impediment to liberty,
dream of a technocratic meritocracy, and see in the new
technologies the basis for a more efficient replacement
for traditional electoral processes.[127] In this new media
environment of abundance, the need for a public broadcaster mandated to serve minority interests and tastes and
to ensure quality service across program genres is by no
means obsolete. The idea that the vastness and diversity
of the Internet, however useful in so many respects, will
somehow provide a satisfactory substitute for the single-
minded dedication to national public service provided by
a public broadcaster (on whatever platform) is untenable;
corporate voices remain the loudest, even on the Internet.

All of this must be kept in mind when thinking about
any public broadcaster's online or new media role. Certainly, whatever the CBC does on the Web, it should
maintain its over-the-air, linear broadcast capacity for
the foreseeable future. At this stage of technological
evolution, nothing can replace traditional broadcasting's
public-service role. Streaming classical music twenty-
four hours a day with no introductions or comment by
informed presenters in no way replaces what was being
done by Radio 2 before the format conversion of 2008,

or is currently being done by Ici Musique. The same can be said about any other musical genre: streaming content in this way ignores the CBC's mandate to expand public taste; to educate and inform, and not just entertain, its audience. And on television, for all its shortcomings, CBC TV is the only English-language broadcaster presenting a full menu of content produced in Canada by Canadians.

Nor has the mass audience of yore entirely disappeared. Richard Nielsen's "congregation" is re-emerging, as television reasserts its dominance in our cultural lives with the serialized, original productions of subscription television services like HBO, Showtime, AMC, Netflix and Amazon Prime. What these very popular productions have in common is a commitment to cinema-level quality, and an absence of commercial interruptions. A properly funded, ad-free CBC/Radio-Canada could compete in this market (in both languages), as the BBC is already doing with series such as *Broadchurch, Wolf Hall* and *Sherlock*. Hockey need not be the only CBC programming that brings Canadians together in front of their screens in large numbers for a shared cultural experience.

A SUPPLEMENTAL SERVICE

But the Web can be used in many ways to supplement and enhance the more traditional services of the public broadcaster. To begin with, the ability of smartphones and tablets to access data wirelessly has meant that, for the first time, television can be truly portable in the same way that radio, with its smaller, simpler receivers, has always been. Watching the Stanley Cup Final or the concluding episode of *Mad Men* on a small smartphone screen may not be ideal, but it beats missing it. And you can do it virtually anywhere in the world. Web-based news can be revised and updated continuously, and the popular cbc.ca news service acts as one of a handful of reliable and impartial sources of brand-name news in the vast morass of unreliable blog-based speculation and commentary.

Of course, the Web enables audience interaction of many kinds, including, for example, voting during elimination reality programs like *Battle of the Blades,* and sharing comments with friends via messaging services like Google Hangouts or on social media. It is assumed that these kinds of interactive features strengthen audience involvement with television programming in general, but it will be some time before research can confirm or debunk this theory. Meanwhile, the Web also provides an environment for experimenting with entirely new ways to package and distribute information, and with new forms of entertainment. Web-based programming of any genre can be produced and distributed at relatively low cost, incorporating audience interaction features impossible in traditional broadcasting. For these reasons, the Web is increasingly being used to test-market television pilots. There's no telling what creative minds may make of the opportunities provided by new technologies, and among the responsibilities of the public broadcaster is to be at the leading edge of this experimentation, taking risks where commercial broadcasters won't.

The immense storage capacity and instantaneous accessibility of digital media means that audio and video programming of all kinds can be archived and made freely accessible, as can important texts and documents. The CBC, in cooperation with other public institutions such as archives, libraries, art galleries, and museums, can aspire to be not only a public broadcaster, but the nation's memory bank, a cumulative, continually expanding archive of Canadian culture, freely available everywhere, on demand, at minimal cost. This archival capacity is an enormously valuable—and just plain enormous—undertaking, and it requires substantial capital and curatorial resources: a lot more money, people and equipment than are currently available at the CBC.[128] It is not a role that any profit-seeking enterprise could be expected to take on, or to adequately fulfill, but it is a natural role for a public-service institution like the CBC, mandated to inform, educate, and entertain its public with "all that is best in every department of human knowledge, endeavour, and achievement." Such a databank would provide a trove of material for future radio and television producers of every genre.

As in conventional broadcasting, the CBC's role on the Web at cbc.ca is one of providing service to the public rather than to advertisers. That service ought to be distinguished by its quality, and that means above all intelligence, reliability, and responsibility. The Web, with its burgeoning blogosphere, is a Wild West of worthwhile content, conspiracy theories, salacious gossip, propaganda, character assassination, vituperation, half-truths, and misinformation of all kinds. What passes for news is often nothing more than endlessly regurgitated rumour and unsubstantiated "fact" seeded by public relations consultants. So-called "iterative journalism," in which half-baked stories are published on blogs and then endlessly commented upon and "refined" by readers, is the opposite of a responsible journalism that strives, through research, direct observation, and dogged investigation, to produce a body of reliable fact—a first draft of history.

It is clear that the impact of advertising on Web content of all kinds, but especially blogs, is even more pronounced than it is in conventional broadcast media. The blogosphere is driven, for the most part, by advertising, and is, if anything, more obsessed with ratings (hits or page views) than conventional radio and television. Its production model—indeed, its entire economic structure—is built on the premise that popularity equals success, and success recursively testifies to quality. Most of the ads on blogs pay the blogger according to the numbers of page views, and search engines are configured to favour keywords in current circulation. Thus, bloggers, whether self-employed or working for sites like Gawker.com or Huffington Post, are advised to focus on currently popular topics and to construe their headlines and text in the most controversial, sensational way they can.[129]

CBC currently sees its digital offerings, including its innovative CBC Player app, as a potentially important source of advertising revenue, and is actively engaged in finding ways to please sponsors with innovative kinds of product placement and embedding.[130] If the CBC is to continue along this path, it needs to develop a strict and transparent code governing how and when advertising will be allowed to intrude in the public broadcaster's on-line offerings. At a minimum, advertising should not be permitted to interfere with access to content (as in forcing users to view a commercial prior to a program) or to interrupt content. But the elimination of advertising would open the way for the CRTC to eliminate data charges for all downloads originating with the pubic broadcaster. This would be a step in the direction of universal accessibility for the PSB, there would be no direct financial harm done to commercial broadcasters, and it would help to distinguish PSB programming from commercial content in the public mind, ameliorating the search problem.

It needs to be remembered that historically, successive new technologies of communication do not replace earlier technologies, but supplement them. Radio did not replace the telephone, television did not replace radio, and so on. Digital technology provides new appliances for the creation, storage and retrieval of all kinds of media content, but it does not replace earlier platforms, or the ways in which audiences relate to them and use them. There will, for the foreseeable future, be both a need and a strong demand for traditional media, and the public-service vocation of the CBC and other public broadcasters will be more valuable, and more necessary, than ever.

In fact, television viewing in Canada has remained remarkably consistent over the past fifteen years, even showing a slight increase with the advent of high-definition, 3-D, and large, flat-screen devices.[131] Internet use climbed steeply over the same period, but seems to be levelling off at about ten hours a week, less than half of the average TV viewing time (with perhaps a quarter of that spent viewing video).[132] About half of those surveyed in recent polls still say they get most of their news from TV, down from sixty percent a decade ago, and spend less than half an hour a week gleaning news and information on the Web. (Google and Facebook each account for more Internet use than all news and information sites combined.) As Canadian Media Research Inc.'s Barry Kiefl notes, "This means that Canadians spend only about thirty minutes per week with news and information Internet sites, Canadian as well as foreign. The *Globe and Mail*'s Web site, or cbc.ca, account for a tiny fraction [of that time] each representing about 1/500th of all time spent using the Internet in Canada, and therefore are unlikely in their present form ever to have the same impact as their print or broadcast versions."[133]

DELIVERY BY INTERNET

The job of a public broadcaster on the Web is twofold: first, to provide citizens, its constituency, with an island of taste, responsibility, and intelligence in this widening sea of "truthiness," prevarication, and provocation. Secondly, its job is to identify and develop those aspects of Web-based media that are most capable of providing a useful service, as this technology, still in its infancy, continues its chaotic and undisciplined development.

Though the transition may be more gradual than some observers have predicted (or some participants had hoped for) the CBC and private broadcasters will both eventually have to adjust to the unfolding reality of the migration of television and radio to the Internet. These services may technically fall within the Broadcasting Act's definition of "broadcasting," and thus, in principle, be subject to CRTC regulation. This is the CRTC's position, and in announcing (in 1999) that it would not regulate Internet-based services, it reserved the right to do so in future. That "right" was reiterated ten years later, and again in 2014, still with no new regulations imposed. The issue of whether the CRTC's regulatory jurisdiction will withstand scrutiny is significant. The trend in OTT services seems to be toward providing an ever-expanding library of not just movies, but regular television fare such as first-run dramatic and sitcom series. These services pose a threat to conventional commercial television's basic business model of buying American programs at a steep discount and delivering them to Canadian audiences, complete with Canadian commercials. It is worth noting, for example, that Netflix's market capitalization of $27 billion in 2015 was many times the combined worth of all Canadian commercial broadcasting entities, which means it has plenty of resources to outbid Canadian networks on any given property and make it available at below cable cost to Canadian OTT subscribers.

It is difficult to see how the CRTC can regulate this business in order to protect the financial interests of commercial television broadcasters, or to impose a tax similar to that paid by conventional cable operators, directed to the development of Canadian content. At the same time, it is possible to see private Canadian broadcasters succumbing to competition from OTT providers, quitting the conventional broadcasting business and joining the enemy. In late 2014, Rogers and Shaw announced a jointly owned Netflix competitor called Shomi, and Bell Media launched Crave, a similar library-based product. But a request to the CRTC that year for permission to shut down over-the-air transmitters at some conventional television stations, in favour of sending their content directly to cable, was denied.[134] It is probably accurate to say that the only thing keeping most of Canada's privately owned commercial television stations in operation as conventional over-the-air outlets is regulation. The biggest economic rewards of the industry have moved elsewhere.

A CONVERGENT FUTURE FOR RADIO, TELEVISION

The convergence of traditional analog media into a common digital format, deliverable through the same wireless and wireline conduits, to the same receiving devices (laptops, tablets, smartphones), makes any discussion of the roles of radio and television in public broadcasting increasingly anachronistic. We tend to think of technologies as replacing one another, but, as noted earlier, that's not what happens with communications technology. Radio should not be dismissed as obsolescent; it could well be the foundation for the future. In the same way, television should not be thought of in terms of an obsolescent model of network-scheduled programs aimed at a mass audience in the home. Radio's great strengths have always been its intimacy and portability: it's a companion. Television has traditionally expected its audience to sit down in one place and watch; it's a tyrant that monopolizes attention. But today, neither of these stereotypes holds true. With Internet distribution, radio can have pictures, and television can be watched on a smartphone.

Increasingly, television—commercial, subscription and public service— has been focusing on its strengths, as the medium that can bring theatre and spectacle into the home, in a form that transcends traditional cinema. The quality miniseries, dramatic or documentary, expands the traditional ninety-minute movie into three or four hours or more, allowing for more expansive, richer, more detailed, and often more honest storytelling, while new high-definition television appliances provide unprecedented picture quality on ever-larger screens. That is where the future of television lies, and where CBC ought to be aiming. This is where the public broadcaster's sought-after audience-as-congregation can still be found.

Radio excels as a low-cost, intimate, always-there,

portable, provider of information, music, and light entertainment. It can now make itself even more attractive by adding video to its repertoire. Programming designed to be watched and/or listened to on portable devices with small screens, like tablets and phones, does not require costly, high-concept production techniques and the associated studios and equipment to be satisfying to its audience. This is true of both information and entertainment genres. A medium formerly known as radio could well provide a new, blended, environment for video-supplemented radio and network TV's traditional news, information, and light entertainment functions, while television moves upscale to explore its own, unlimited, cinematic potential.

CHAPTER 10

REVITALIZING THE CBC

The cornerstone legislation governing media in Canada is old enough in Internet years to qualify as neolithic. The Broadcasting Act was passed in 1991, and since then the media landscape has been radically altered by new technologies and by political realities. The Act's basic assumption that public service is to be the guiding principle of all broadcasting, public and private. Its requirement that all broadcasting be "predominantly Canadian," with the CBC acting as the "distinctively Canadian" foundation of the system, has been so badly eroded through regulatory change and political neglect that it is today irrelevant and immaterial.[135] Where the CBC was once seen as the vital cornerstone of the Canadian broadcasting industry, it has become an appendage (except in Quebec), under constant threat of irrelevance or total extinction. But while the picture painted in preceding chapters portrays daunting challenge to the CBC, it may also expose a rare political opportunity for revitalization.

First of all, given the current and ongoing state of ownership concentration in Canadian media, in which five vertically integrated corporations earn about ninety percent of total industry revenue, the public broadcaster is quite clearly the only bulwark against monopoly control and its noxious effect on service delivery of all kinds.[136] This anti-monopoly, pro-market argument for the continued existence of a public broadcaster is one that ought to be politically attractive within the context of neo-liberal economic ideology, which sees monopolies as being fatal to the healthy functioning of markets. Monopoly is anathema to laissez-faire liberalism.

Next, there is the pervasive culture of public subsidies to commercial media interests, another area of interference in the free functioning of media markets that runs counter to liberal market theory. While a case can be made within liberal economic theory for public provision of services that the market cannot or will not provide (technically, "public goods"), subsidies to commercial interests operating in a competitive market amount to governments picking winners and losers, another sin against neo-liberal fundamentalism. The Canadian broadcasting industry has been replete with such market-distorting government subsidies to commercial interests since the very earliest days of radio. Not only did the CRBC provide several hours of free programming a day to its private affiliates, it paid for the wireline delivery charges, and it paid the stations to air it. And the increased audiences that were generated allowed the stations to boost their rate cards!

As well, government investment in the CRBC and its successor the CBC contributed powerfully to the early technical and financial development of a thriving and highly profitable broadcasting industry, first in radio, and then in television. When television was launched in 1952 – 1953, the CBC once again provided a backbone of programming for a rapidly growing number of private stations, making most of them instantly profitable. In those early years, private stations obtained an average of sixty percent of their programming from the CBC; in many cases the proportion ran to eighty-five percent. The subsidy continued well into the 1960s, at a cost to taxpayers of hundreds of millions of dollars.[137]

More recently, the Conservative government of Brian Mulroney decided in 1984 to replace the Canadian Film Development Corporation with a new crown corporation called Telefilm Canada. Telefilm was to oversee public subsidies for Canadian content in both film and television programming, and in the process it has effectively transformed the CBC from a program producer to a commissioner of programs made by independent, for-profit production houses. Private producers welcomed the removal of their chief competition from the marketplace, though they have since had reason to reflect on their early enthusiasm. According to one experienced producer, "Prior to [Telefilm] and similar funds, broadcasters (large and small) built, maintained and bore the burden of the cost of facilities (studios, cameras, lights, props, costumes, etc.) as well as the manpower and production costs related to whatever programming they produced…. Under the current model, the vast majority of the burden of financing facilities, equipment, office, professional services, talent, catering, transportation, etc., etc., has been offloaded onto the independent producers, along with said producers being responsible for finding the vast majority of the funding … from multiple sources." In the end, "the winners of this arrangement are: the broadcasters who now shoulder much less than the traditional cost of production (lead broadcasters supply as little as 5%); the banks that 'bridge finance' the producers until the producers actually get their payments from broadcasters, the grant agencies, the sponsors and the funds; the distributors who benefit indirectly from the production being created for them to market abroad; and last and often least, the [independent] producers."[138]

Between 1991 and 2009, while the federal government's expenditure on CBC/Radio-Canada rose by only eight percent, federal subsidies to private, commercial broadcasters rose by somewhere between forty-eight and fifty-nine percent, depending on how the calculation is done. These subsidies came partly in the form of advertising substitution regulations (sim-sub), which require broadcasters to replace American ads with Canadian advertising in US programming they purchase and simulcast in over-the-air transmissions. In 2014 the value of this subsidy was estimated to be between $242 and $262 million annually.[139]

There's more. Section 19.1 of the federal Income Tax Act prohibits Canadian businesses from deducting, as an expense for income tax purposes, any advertisements they might place on foreign broadcasters that are "directed primarily to a market in Canada." The policy was implemented half a century ago to prevent American television and radio stations close to large Canadian urban centres from draining advertising dollars with their cross-border broadcasts. The value of this federal subsidy to Canadian commercial broadcasters was estimated in 2011 to be between $191 and $130 million a year.[140]

Commercial broadcasters can also apply for program development and production subsidies from Telefilm, the federally supported Canadian television production fund that pays out about $200 million a year. In a typical scenario, a network, say CTV, fronts the first twenty percent of production costs for a new series, and that triggers several sources of public monies: funding of up to fifteen percent from the Canadian Media Fund (run jointly by the Department of Canadian Heritage and the cable industry, and administered by Telefilm, and up to forty-nine percent funding from Telefilm itself. Public subsidies thus can account for up to about eighty percent of a network's production costs. (The CBC is also eligible for this funding.) The estimated value of this subsidy for private broadcasters is $177 million a year. Special tax relief for Canadian productions, adds about $520 million to the annual production subsidy.

Federal subsidies for private broadcasters as detailed here amount to between $1 and $1.1 billion annually. The CBC's Parliamentary appropriation in 2015 was $783 million.

But there's still more: in 2007, the CRTC responded to pleas from private television stations hard hit by the Great Recession by setting up an emergency fund for the production of newscasts and other local programming in non-metropolitan markets. The money came from a mandatory tax on cable and satellite signal providers of one percent of revenue, a cost that most of these providers immediately passed on to their customers, so that the fund was in effect paid for by cable and satellite subscribers. In 2011, eighty local private stations received $106 million from this pool of money; over the life of the fund, it had paid out roughly $600 million in subsidies. It was discontinued in 2014.

The ostensible purpose of lavishing government largesse on private television production is to encourage the commercial networks to produce more Canadian content to offset the hundreds of millions of dollars they spend on American programs each year. And it has done that. However, commercial networks do what they do to make profit, and profit is maximized when this heavily subsidized Can-con is also sold in foreign markets. The result has been that many of the Canadian television programs produced with Telefilm money are scarcely recognizable as Canadian on the screen, a feature that makes them easier to sell abroad. The values they embody are not so much Canadian as commercial. Furthermore, commercial networks tend to air their Canadian content in off-peak viewing hours, leaving prime time to their more lucrative American imports (and thus reaping sim-sub revenue).

The federal subsidies paid to private Canadian broadcasters raise an obvious question: why should Canadian taxpayers funnel money to a handful of highly profitable media conglomerates whose television networks (a small part of their business) finance themselves by rebroadcasting American television shows, and which relegate their mandatory Canadian quotas to newscasts and off-peak viewing hours? Why not instead adequately fund the nation's public broadcaster, which owes its fiduciary responsibility to the nation's citizens rather than to corporate shareholders?

NECESSARY BALANCE

We live in an era of epic challenges, both national and global, arising out of financial instability, geopolitical transformations, environmental calamity, massive migrations of desperate human populations, religious animus, terrorism, the threat of nuclear weapons, and runaway developments in science and technology. That much is conventional wisdom. What is not so well understood is that, due to these challenges and many others, there has never been greater need for the kind of thoughtful dialogue and considered judgment that can take place only in public spaces. The most important of spaces is our media, and in particular public media, which by definition are a public preserve intended to be safe from influences by vested interests, governmental or commercial.

There was a time when all broadcasting was understood by both the public and the industry's entrepreneurs to involve a degree of public service, thought of either as a moral responsibility or simply a payback for permission to use the public airwaves. That era of media came to an end beginning in the 1980s with the rise of neo-liberalism and the messianic belief in the moral authority of unfettered market capitalism. If we can judge from such manifestations of social disaffection as the Occupy movement, we now appear to be entering a phase of reaction to this, of regret over the destruction of so much social value embodied in the public-service initiatives of the great commercial media organizations of the middle decades of the twentieth century. It seems highly doubtful, however, that the clock can be turned back where the mammoth corporate media conglomerates are concerned—they have become too big and powerful and politically potent to be persuaded to forego profit in favour of a renewal of their public-service mission. No professionally managed television network, for example, will voluntarily decide to restore its spending on news and current affairs to pre-deregulation levels simply because it's the right thing to do. The laser-like focus in these organizations is on their fiduciary responsibility to shareholders.

Clearly, the public-service assumptions (though not

the prescriptions) of Canada's Broadcasting Act of 1991 are outdated. Yet if we can no longer rely on commercial media to serve the public interest beyond some minimal entertainment function, we can at least insist that they entertain us responsibly. In this country there remains a body of regulation administered mainly by the CRTC that prevents broadcasting from descending to quite the depths plumbed in some of the news commentary and reality programming seen in the US. There are no equivalents to *Extreme Makeover* or the *Rush Limbaugh Show* being perpetrated here: to do so would put broadcasting licences in jeopardy. And we are fortunate to still have more than a remnant of true public-service broadcasting in CBC/Radio-Canada. We have a strong rootstock on which to begin to grow a new system more suited to the media ecology of the twenty-first century as defined by our current political, economic, social, and technological realities. If we can no longer depend on commercial broadcasters to educate and enlighten in any significant way, or to challenge us with groundbreaking entertainment, the CBC is entirely capable of filling those public interest gaps. What the CBC needs is a sustainable, predictable level of public funding, and a management culture in which the goals of public -service broadcasting are understood and there is a willingness to achieve these goals. All of this can be realized, but there must first be public recognition that the provision of public space for the cultural discourse that will shape our future is too important to be left in the hands of a small coterie of profit-driven corporate oligopolists.

AN ACTION PLAN: FINANCE

Advertising is incompatible, both in principle and in practice, with public-service broadcasting, for reasons detailed in the preceding chapters. Revitalization, then, must begin with the elimination of advertising on CBC across all conventional broadcast platforms. In the non-linear online environment, advertising may be acceptable, but only if it is never embedded in content and made impossible to avoid. If advertising were eliminated from the CBC, a substantial portion of the more than $400 million in ad revenue collected annually by the CBC would become available to private broadcasters, who have for nearly a century complained bitterly about competition for advertising dollars from the public broadcaster. If the CBC were to end commercial sponsorship, private stations would see a substantial increase in revenue both from increased ad rates and reductions in unsold inventory. Some of that windfall could be directed to news and other Canadian content. Furthermore, according to the CRTC, the CBC spends $136 million a year on sales and promotion: industry insiders estimate about $100 million of that goes to support its advertising sales department, with its hundreds of agents.[141] This is money that could be spent on programming.

The federal government must substantially increase the CBC/Radio-Canada annual parliamentary appropriation, which is currently less than $1 billion, as an investment in the nation's democratic future. Canadians spend annually about $28 per capita funding their public broadcaster; the average of sixteen nations surveyed by Nordicity in 2013 was $82 per capita. For CBC/Radio-Canada's funding to reach that average—not an ambitious target given the country's vast territory, its proximity to the Hollywood juggernaut, and its bilingual, multicultural aspirations—funding would have be almost tripled. This should be a medium-term target. Given the political and economic realities of Canada's communications industries, if high-quality Canadian entertainment and information programming is to be produced in adequate quantity across program types and delivery platforms, it will have to be done mainly by the public broadcaster. The market failure where these important public goods are concerned is real and needs to be resolved, and only a properly funded public-service broadcaster can fix it. Private subsidies have been tried and have failed to do the job.

A national public broadcaster is not a frill: it's basic infrastructure. As such, it needs to be maintained, and that costs money. Ottawa has avoided making this necessary investment for too long. The federal subsidy for CBC/Radio-Canada was the same in 2015 as it was in 1991, which means, when inflation is taken into account, it had been reduced by half. (Over the same period, funding for the BBC tripled.) The mandate specified in the Broadcasting Act, however, has not changed. The result is, as one might expect, that this vital piece of infrastructure is danger of collapse.

As the CBC and its supporters search with growing

urgency for solutions to the public broadcaster's critical funding problems, an idea gaining some traction is that CBC Television be dismantled and spun off into a clutch of subscription-based cable specialty channels. That way, viewers could select what they want to subscribe to, rather than paying for the public broadcaster as a monolithic institution. Their subscription fees would eliminate the need for advertising, which most advocates agree is antithetical to the goals of public-service broadcasting.

It's an idea that has strong initial appeal. For one thing, it would mean that those who weren't interested in watching the public broadcaster's programming wouldn't have to pay for it. Right now, every Canadian taxpayer contributes to the CBC/Radio-Canada's federal subsidy. And economists like to point out that subscriber-based TV has the advantage of providing an indicator of consumers' preferences, through pricing signals. People will pay more for content they like a lot; programmers can use this feedback to tailor their offerings. Furthermore, where producers of any product are isolated from market signals such as pricing (or audience ratings) they're apt to lose touch with consumers and fail to satisfy their preferences. That's all standard-issue market dogma.

Unfortunately it doesn't make much sense when applied to a commodity like public-service broadcasting. To understand why, one need only think of public education, another public good. What would happen if we let the market decide what our universities placed on offer? Business and engineering schools might do all right because there's a high probability of an immediate payback to the investment in tuition, but English, philosophy, political science, psychology, sociology, astronomy, experimental physics—the pure sciences, the social sciences, and the humanities—would wither away for lack of support. Society supports the arts and humanities and the pure sciences because there's an obvious, market-overriding benefit to doing so. In television, there are many areas of worthwhile programming where the potential audience is too small or too specialized in its interests to be attractive to for-profit producers. Successful subscription-based services like HBO restrict their offerings to a few popular genres, in the interests of maximizing their subscriber base and the revenue it produces.

Any public broadcaster forced to rely exclusively, or even in part, on subscriber fees would quickly find itself in a dilemma: whether to produce exclusively mainstream, revenue-generating programming and thus ensure the organization's survival, or risk viability by producing more challenging programs that serve wider, deeper, more diverse, interests. In other words, whether to look to the bottom line, or serve the public. (This is essentially the identical problem CBC Television has had to wrestle with, in its current hybrid public/commercial form.)

In strict financial terms, the specialty-channel model simply doesn't fly. There are about twelve million cable-subscribing households in Canada, so for the CBC/Radio-Canada to be funded to a level close to the OECD average, it would need to raise about $2.5 billion from

that subscriber base each year—a monthly bill per subscriber of about $17, assuming everybody signed up for
all the CBC offerings. If half of cabled households chose
to subscribe to the full range of channels—an optimistic forecast—each of those subscribers would have to be
charged more than $34 a month to keep the service afloat.
That would be in addition to the current average Canadian household cable/wireless bill of between $165 and
$185 a month (depending on the range of services). The
only reliable research into whether Canadians would be
willing to pay more on their cable bills for better quality
programming, conducted by Canadian Media Research
Inc. over the past decade, has consistently shown that
only about forty percent of respondents would be willing
to pay even an extra $5 a month.[142]

Non-subscribers would furthermore be shut out of
the public broadcaster's offerings, even on the rare occasions when they might want to watch, such as in cases of
national emergency, or celebration. For a public broadcaster, this is a deal-breaker. The Pilkington Committee
report on public broadcasting in the UK addressed this
point definitively half a century ago: "To finance the
Corporation in whole or in part from the proceeds of the
sale—to those who want and can afford them—of particular programme items would … positively discourage
and make more difficult the provision of a balanced service. We reject, therefore, as opposed to the purpose of
public-service broadcasting, the idea that the BBC should
engage in subscription television."[143]

Some CBC advocates have argued that the public broadcaster could be financed by corporate and private philanthropy, like PBS and NPR in the United States. That too is a badly flawed model. American public broadcasting, which relies heavily on charitable donations, has found itself seriously compromised when important donors have threatened to withdraw their funding over objections to programming decisions.[144] The basic infrastructure of a democratic society should not be funded by philanthropy.

For the CBC/Radio-Canada to continue to exist as a true public broadcaster, it must be funded by what accountants call actuarial means: everybody contributes the same small amount to the pot, regardless of how much they take out in terms of the amount of programming consumed. That way, the service is there for everybody, whenever they need or want it, like the public-school system and medicare. The actuarial system recognizes that all Canadians benefit from the existence of a public-service broadcaster that provides high-quality information, education, and entertainment programming—whether or not they use those services themselves—in the same way as they benefit from a good public school system, whether or not they have children. It makes the country a better place to live and work.

The current funding model for the CBC accepts this actuarial premise, to a degree, providing an annual appropriation to the public broadcaster drawn from general revenues. The problem is that this money is doled out at the discretion of the government of the day, and funding cuts have been frequent and seemingly arbitrary. In order to fill the gap between its mandated obligations and its funding, the CBC has for much of its history had to supplement its annual appropriation with advertising revenue.

A better solution is a small levy on the profits of the handful of enormously profitable companies that supply our commercial television, cable, and broadband services in a regulated, oligopolistic market environment—the nation's BDUs. A levy of five to seven percent on the revenues of Bell, Rogers, Shaw, Telus, and Quebecor would raise roughly $3.5 billion, the equivalent of $100 per capita, enough to fund the CBC/Radio-Canada at levels that would allow it to join the ranks of the world's most successful and highly regarded public broadcasters.

Of course the money needed to properly resource the public broadcaster could in principle be taken straight out of general revenues. But the highly integrated media and telecommunications industry in Canada is awash in money—revenues soared past $62 billion in 2014[145]— and could well afford a small surcharge on profits to support this necessary piece of infrastructure, which prevents the worst effects of market monopoly and resolves a serious market failure. The cost to BDUs would inevitably be added to their customers' monthly bills, where it would scarcely be noticed: Canadians already spend more than $3,000 a year on their telecom, cable, and satellite television services. It would be, in effect, a more efficient version of the license fee on radio and television appliances that has carried the BBC successfully through to the present day.

WHAT TO DO ABOUT SPORTS

Hockey Night in Canada, which celebrated its sixtieth anniversary in 2014, was for much of its history the CBC's most watched show. Playoff audiences sometimes topped five million. NHL hockey was also the network's biggest moneymaker, bringing in an annual haul of about $100 million, roughly a third of total CBC advertising revenue. Many other public broadcasters carry professional sports. The BBC, for example, spends just under one-tenth of its public subsidy on sports rights, including soccer, justifying the expense by arguing that major sporting events can bring communities, and the nation, together; sports broadcasts are enjoyed by audiences that are otherwise underserved by the public broadcaster, such as young men, lower-income, and ethnic minority audiences. In other words, professional sport broadcasting can help public broadcasters fulfill the mandate of reaching all segments of the population with excellent programming they enjoy and want to watch. By the time CBC lost the rights to NHL hockey to Rogers Media in 2014, it was clear that the franchise had become an albatross around the public broadcaster's neck. It had to go.

Like the BBC, in a normal (non-Olympic) year CBC/Radio-Canada was in the habit of spending about one-tenth of its annual revenue on sports, about $150 million. Most of this (approximately eighty percent) went to NHL hockey and *Hockey Night in Canada*. Marketing expenses added substantially to that cost, as much as $20 million. Revenue was $100 million; expenses $140 million. Hockey produced a substantial net loss. During the October-to-June season, hockey accounted for up to 400 hours of CBC television programming, all of it Canadian content. Considering the BBC's rationale for broadcasting pro sports, it could be argued that 400 hours is not a disproportionate allocation of time. The CBC could well claim that this is what it takes to engage those young men, low-income earners and ethnic minorities it would otherwise fail to reach. However, the BBC is able to spread its sports coverage over two television channels (BBC 1 and 2), its Radio 5 live news and sports outlet, and its online services, while CBC's sports programming was confined to its one English-language television channel and cbc. ca. (Radio-Canada relinquished French-language NHL hockey rights to the private cable sports outlet RDS in 2001.) The result was that NHL hockey alone consumed a whopping forty percent of the prime-time schedule on CBC TV between October and May. Clearly, this was a serious programming imbalance.

The other problem was the advertising: CBC could not afford pro hockey, even at an annual net loss, without commercial sponsorship. Hockey, more than any other program genre, forced CBC to remain in the advertising/ratings game. The BBC, on the other hand, has enough revenue to pay for rights to key events and series, and its sportscasts contain no advertising: the BBC ran the 2012 Olympics as host broadcaster, without commercial sponsorship.[146]

One less obvious issue with sports and the ad revenue it generates for CBC is hidden in statistics collected by the CRTC on CBC TV program expenditures across categories: foreign; drama/comedy; other Canadian; sports; news and information. These data show that in 2014 the public broadcaster spent $236 million on sports, including its FIFA World Cup and Sochi Olympic games programming, compared to $125 million the previous (non-Olympic, non-FIFA World Cup) year. What is revealing is the amount spent on drama/comedy in those two years: $85 million in the non-Olympic/FIFA year of 2013, and just $61 million in the big sports year of 2014. Clearly, the decision to produce Sochi and the World Cup cost drama production dearly—$24 million.

The difficulty with the CBC carrying no professional sports, not even the iconic events, is that the big, vertically integrated BDUs like Rogers that do carry them are able to siphon off key games and series to their subscription-only specialty channels, where producers glean revenue from both advertisements and subscription fees. This happened long ago, for instance, with the Canadian Football League's Grey Cup playoffs. In the UK, broadcast regulations stipulate that listed events deemed to be of national interest—the FIFA World Cup, Wimbledon, the Olympics, the Grand National and others—must be made available without subscription fee (that is, over-the-air) to ninety-five percent of the nation, a policy that guarantees the BBC rights to carriage since only they have the necessary terrestrial coverage. These are described as "events of national resonance that bring the nation together."

In Canada, a similar arrangement for guaranteeing universal access would require the creation of a list of sports events of national significance by the Department of Canadian Heritage. Live coverage of listed events would be required to be made available to all Canadians, over-the-air and via basic cable. The rights holders would not lose money under such an arrangement even if they chose to broadcast the event from behind a paywall, on a subscription channel. They would instead stand to gain, since the added free-riding viewers would enlarge the overall audience, raising the value of advertising spots, and thus profit. For a future advertising-free CBC/Radio-Canada to participate would require a special exemption for these events, granted by the CRTC. It should be a goal of he CBC/Radio-Canada to seek such an arrangement.

CAN-CON: IF NOT THE CBC, THEN WHO?

Part of the difficulty in trying to predict the evolution of broadcasting is a tendency to conflate programming and delivery platforms. Phrases like "the golden age of radio" embody this habit. In the new world of digital convergence, in which all media are produced, stored and delivered on the same computer-based technologies, and can be delivered to the same multi purpose devices, from laptops to notebooks to smartphones, it no longer make sense to talk of radio and television, or for that matter, newspapers, as if they were essentially different media. Today, television can be as intimate and portable as radio, radio can have video, and your daily newspaper carries video and audio clips along with its print stories on the Web.

The useful distinctions would seem to involve screen size and portability. In principle, all information content, including movies, can be accessed on a smartphone. And you could read your email or watch YouTube cat videos on your eighty-five-inch plasma-screen home theatre, should you care to. Realistically, television's destiny is home cinema, where it has already transcended century-old boundaries of moviemaking. And radio will take on all the mundane chores that for three-quarters of a century have been shared by portable, intimate, radio, and box-in-the-living-room television: the news and information, short documentaries, soaps, sitcoms, and light entertainment that traditionally distinguished television from movies.

In this new media environment, there are cost savings to be had in what was formerly television production, because technical production values need not be as high. Delivery will eventually no longer involve expensive over-the-air transmitters; content will be fed directly to the Internet. CBC has begun doing encouraging exploratory work in this area with low definition TV versions of the radio programs *q* and *Canada Reads*.

Production costs for the big multi-episode cinematic

blockbusters will necessarily be much higher than for a standard television program. But there is reason to believe that high-quality, genuinely Canadian content can be sold abroad to recoup some costs. Why would multi-part series labelled, for example, *The Masseys*, or *La Vérendrye,* or *Blackberry*, or *Leonard*, or *Greenpeace,* if produced to the highest international standards, not sell on international markets?

In the 1960s and 1970s, cutting-edge CBC television productions made for the domestic market were aired worldwide, including on the BBC, and the corporation's producers and directors were in hot demand in Hollywood and London. Historian Mary Jane Miller has warned that both the institution and the nation are damaged by our failure to remember these early glory days:

> Too often, the CBC hides or throws away its accomplishments, downgrades its practitioners, suffers from cultural amnesia about its own past ... The fact is that cultural amnesia can be fatal unless memory and reflection, however selective or flawed, reverse the deterioration of the body politic. *Je me souviens*—I remember—is, as Quebecers already know, the only way for a culture and a country to survive.[147]

With the exception of its limited remaining documentary capability and its news studios, the current CBC has been essentially stripped of its television production capacity. Experienced producers and directors are scarce today in what was once a place that trained and employed some of the world's great television talents. If the CBC is to play a part in the burgeoning golden age of television, there seems no realistic option, in the short term, other than for the corporation to act as a commissioning agent for new television production. To ensure that these productions are authentically Canadian, it would be necessary for the CBC to fund independent producers to a level that would make it unnecessary for them to target international sales as a first priority, as is the case today. The market, left to its own dynamics, simply will not produce indigenous Can-con—if it is to exist, it must be created, or at least commissioned and sponsored, by the public broadcaster.

The devolution of the CBC from producer-broadcaster to commissioner-publisher got underway in earnest amid the neo-liberal zeal that gripped western nations in the closing decades of the twentieth century. The 1982 Applebaum-Hébert report on federal cultural policy had recommended the breaking up of the CBC and shuttering the National Film Board of Canada: agreeing to outsource half of its production to independents was the corporation's defensive response, justified in public as a way to introduce greater diversity of voices in program offerings, to support and help develop the independent film production industry, and above all, to save money. Save money it did, by forcing artists and craftspeople of all descriptions into the precarious world of independent film-making, where employment is sporadic, wages are relatively low, and job security and benefits are a chimera. Ignoring the ethical issues raised, it is possible to ask whether or not there is a threshold in size and what might be termed creative density beyond which an enterprise like the CBC cannot fall without an irretrievable loss of identity and functionality. Commenting on efforts in the UK to reduce or eliminate in-house productions at the BBC, media scholar Michael Tracey warns of triggering "a kind of cultural anorexia. There is an important, but highly abstract and intangible, argument that successful public broadcasters tend to be 'large-ish', with sufficient creative mass to fund, nurture, and give space to talent across a range of genres. Shrink that size too far and the institution becomes impoverished."[148]

NEW LEADERSHIP

A great broadcasting enterprise ought to be run by people steeped at some level in the practice of producing great programming. A great public broadcaster needs leadership profoundly committed to the goals and values of public service.

Successive federal governments, from Mackenzie King's Liberals down to Stephen Harper's Conservatives, had been nervous about the existence of a thriving public-service broadcaster over which they have little control beyond annual subsidy allocations. Newscasts sometimes expose policy blunders or uncover corruption and incompetence. Commentary may be critical of government programs or initiatives. Satire on radio or television can make government figures seem ridiculous. On television, the balance can be somewhat redressed through government "public-service" advertising, and by political attack ads, but on advertising-free radio even that balm is unavailable. Public broadcasting may make for a culturally literate, well-informed public, but it does nothing to make managing politics easier for those in power.

In 2013 the Harper government went a step beyond jerking the financial leash, to providing for direct government involvement in CBC's labour negotiations. The budget that year contained a provision giving Ottawa bureaucrats—and through them Cabinet—a seat at the bargaining table whenever the CBC is negotiating contracts with its unions. The government's rationale, as expressed in a Treasury Board Press release, was to ensure that taxpayers' money is spent responsibly. The CBC countered that its salaries had gone up at about half the rate of private broadcasters' over the previous seven year. Others noted that the Broadcasting Act states explicitly that CBC employees are to be dealt with as employees of an independent Crown corporation and not as public servants under government supervision, so as to shield them from political influence. Nevertheless, until challenged in court, the government's involvement in negotiations will extend not just to rates of pay, but to all other contract considerations, including hiring policy and working conditions, and it will include hiring and remuneration of non-union contract employees as well.

It is difficult to imagine how collective bargaining could take place in good faith if there is a suspicion that the employer's negotiators are puppets of the federal cabinet. Former CBC President Tony Manera has made the crucial point that it's not so much a question of whether the government will use its new powers to try to influence CBC programming, as whether there is a public perception that it does so. This perception is of course especially critical where news is concerned, and in particular news coverage of Parliament. Imagine some future high-profile CBC journalist doing an accountability interview with the Prime Minister, knowing that every aggressive question might put his job with the corporation in peril. If the interview were perceived to have been too soft, what conclusion might the public draw?

The senior management of the CBC has been rendered dysfunctional by political patronage, and needs to be restructured in a way that will put it in the hands of qualified men and women who understand and are sympathetic to the role of public-service broadcasting. Cabinet currently appoints the CBC president. For the past fifty years, these appointments have been drawn almost exclusively from the senior ranks of the federal civil service, with the overwhelming emphasis being on men (they have all been men) who had a firm grasp of accounting. As the veteran producer Richard Nielsen has written:

Canadian broadcasting, like all broadcasting, is an extremely complex industry involving technological innovation; business arrangements that involve foreign countries; production involving sometimes difficult and always challenging artists and producers, and distribution patterns that are constantly changing, all of it involving a rapid pace of technological change. Canada alone seems to have decided that no experience whatsoever is required in conducting and leading such a corporation.

He adds, ruefully: "I've known and had dealings with practically all the Presidents beginning with Alphonse Ouimet [appointed 1957] and they were honourable and intelligent men who with few exceptions left their posts as ignorant as they had arrived, proving that Ottawa is not a good vantage point from which to understand the industry nor is it an industry that can be learned from the top."[149] Successive federal governments have seen the role of president of the CBC as involving, principally, the curbing of a perceived propensity for lavish spending, and, from time to time, providing a counterweight in Quebec to separatist sentiments. A "safe hand."

If the CBC is to be allowed to do its job at arm's-length from government and its political preoccupations, the president should be chosen by the corporation's Board of Directors, and should serve at its pleasure. As to the Board of Directors itself, for the past half-century and longer, federal governments have made appointments more on the basis of political alignment than on knowledge of the industry or commitment to the values of public broadcasting.[150] There needs to be a system for appointing board members that is at arm's-length from government. In the UK, this is accomplished by a process designed by the distinguished jurist Lord Nolan in 1995 following a patronage and corruption scandal. The Nolan Rules, as the system has become known worldwide, is a non-partisan selection process that provides for transparency, careful assessment of merit, and oversight by a Commissioner of Public Appointments (who is independent of both civil service and government), in the process of selecting a short list of candidates from which the Minister then makes his or her choice. The system is designed explicitly to eliminate the kind of patronage appointment that has characterized the CBC's board for generations. Some version of it could, and should be, adopted here. The CBC Board of Directors (currently ten persons, plus the CBC/ Radio-Canada president and the chair of the board, all appointed by Cabinet) selected under Nolan Rules would elect a chair from its own ranks, and would then hire a full-time president, or chief executive officer, for the corporation. Alternatively, the board could select a candidate for president and recommend that person to Cabinet for appointment.

One of the benefits of such a non-partisan system of appointments would be that board members, the chair and president would all be in a position to act as public advocates for the CBC, even in the face of government hostility. Predictable long-term findings, as discussed earlier, would reinforce this independence. The other side of the coin is public accountability and transparency, another area in which recent CBC management has been deficient. Decisions to alter programming or services should not come as a surprise to the audience—who are also shareholders—making them feel disenfranchised and alienated. This was a lesson that should have been learned with the disastrous response to funding cuts in the early 1990s. Public consultations could have averted or mitigated the impact of what is now widely accepted to have been a terrible blunder: CBC virtually eliminated the network's regional television services, pulling back from local television news coverage, and closing down eleven stations altogether. This proved to be a disastrous strategic error. It provoked an angry public outcry of startling ferocity, and disaffected audiences in these markets deserted network programming across the entire broadcast schedule. CBC is not a private company, and it is only its current competitive position in the advertising market that justifies the secrecy surrounding its decision-making. Free of advertising, it would be in a position to involve its audiences in making the decisions that affect the services they rely on and care about. Increased participation can only improve the quality of those decisions, while at the same time cultivating loyalty.

SERVING THE PUBLIC

It all comes down to public service.

Advertising was introduced to broadcasting in this country with great reluctance, as it was in the United States. In both countries, the 1920s and 1930s was a time of progressive politics and the idea of public service was an active meme in both business and politics. In America, the resistance to commercials on the airwaves was quickly overcome when clever entrepreneurs invented the business strategy of stringing together nationwide networks of radio stations over long-distance telephone lines, dramatically lowering programming cost for the industry and opening up the country to national advertisers. The revenue potential was simply too great to be ignored. But those network entrepreneurs were creatures of their time, concerned with their good name and willing to trade profit for prestige. Network advertising was confined almost exclusively to sustaining sponsors, who paid for entire programs and series in order to have their brand attached to popular, high-quality entertainment. Out of this arrangement came the excellence nowadays characterized as the golden age of radio.

In Canada, commercial sponsorship was adopted as the only workable way to build a national broadcasting network and provide the kind of high-quality programming being enjoyed by listeners south of the border. Throughout most of the history of Canadian broadcasting, the CBC functioned both as a stand-alone public-service broadcaster, and also a producer of Canadian program- ming, which it supplied to private stations at no cost, in compensation for their risk-taking in setting up radio and television stations throughout the country. The risk, for many, was minimal: the business of regional broadcasting was famously characterized as a licence to print money, as private broadcasters loaded up their schedules with in- expensive American programs and filled blank spots with free CBC fare. Nevertheless, government support for pri- vate, commercial broadcasting in Canada has continued to be a significant part of the institutional structure of the broadcasting industry, as detailed earlier in this chapter.

This no longer makes sense, given the realities of the industry today.

Private broadcasters are no longer local, independent businessmen struggling to make ends meet while provid- ing needed services like local news and weather, com- munity information, and light entertainment to their communities. Private broadcasters today are typically enormous corporate conglomerates like Rogers, Bell, Shaw, Quebecor, and the handful of other, smaller cor- porations that own and control Canadian commercial broadcast media. Commercial broadcasting has become an industry like any other, dominated by professionally managed corporations whose shares are widely held, and which are narrowly focused on maximizing shareholder value. The private industry can no longer reasonably be considered to be pre-eminently a public service; it serves advertisers and shareholders.

History shows that, with few exceptions, pioneer private broadcasters could be counted on to display a sense of public responsibility, because their personal reputations were at stake in their communities. But nobody expects modern corporations to behave this way: their sense of responsibility to the public, as opposed to their shareholders, begins and ends with compliance with law and regulation. The essence of so-called corporate social responsibility lies in obedience to law and regulation (that is, in prudence, rather than virtue), and corporate altruism is necessarily calibrated to offsetting profit derived through improved public reputation and related sales. If we want private broadcasters to serve public-policy ends, such as including a certain level of Canadian content in their broadcast schedules, the responsibility must be imposed through regulation. Even then, it is naive to expect any large, publicly held, and professionally managed corporation to do anything more than comply with the exact letter, as opposed to the spirit, of the law. Loopholes are inevitably found, and must be closed with more rules. This makes the drafting of effective regulations, and their enforcement, exceedingly difficult and often politically unpalatable.

Only a public broadcaster will serve the public interest wholeheartedly and with imagination, creativity, and real enthusiasm. Canada, inescapably bound through communication technologies to the world's biggest exporter of cultural products, cannot afford to be without a vibrant, inventive, relevant CBC.

Canadians need to realize that complex organizations

must maintain a certain size if they are to survive and flourish. Underfunded players in competitive markets tend to be robbed of their most valuable employees, either because morale is poor, or they can't offer sufficiently attractive salaries, or because opportunities are limited in comparison with rival firms. The point has been reached, either by design or neglect, where further cutbacks to the CBC's funding will no longer lead to quantitative tinkering with its output, but to fundamental, qualitative transformation in the organization itself. It will, in future, have increasing difficulty justifying its continued existence.

This ought to be a matter of pressing national concern, because the public broadcaster is a crucial component of the infrastructure of Canada's democracy. It either employs, or gives a platform to, some of the nation's best and brightest minds. The CBC is by consensus Canada's most important cultural institution—in fostering cultural literacy; in providing fair and accurate information and informed, responsible analysis; in addressing the tastes of minorities and the needs of the disenfranchised; in serving its audiences as citizens rather than consumers; and in providing programming of all kinds produced by and for Canadians, it provides an irreplaceable service. If it did not exist, it would have to be invented. But it does exist, albeit in a sadly debilitated form. There are few areas of public policy more in need of urgent attention, or more amenable to straightforward remedies, than the sustaining and enhancement of the CBC/Radio-Canada.

NOTES

INTRODUCTION

1   See Appendix for the CBC mandate.

2   Internal CBC staff memo, March 25, 2015.

3   Mike De Souza, "Senate plans comprehensive review of CBC's role in Canadian society (and how it spends billions in subsidies,)" Postmedia News, Dec. 3, 2013.

4   Angus Reid Institute, http://angusreid.org/canadian-culture.

5   CRTC Policy Monitoring Report. Viewers 2+.

CHAPTER 1

6   NPR, formerly National Public Radio, and PBS, the American Public Broadcasting Service on television, were founded only in 1970, during the presidency of Lyndon B. Johnson. NPR both produces and distributes information and cultural programming, while PBS is primarily a distributor. Both are funded by charitable donations and corporate underwriting in the form of "institutional" advertisements, which cannot include comparisons, or calls to action. The federal Corporation for Public Broadcasting, also established in 1970, provides some minimal funding as well.

7   I have told this story in detail in chapters 14 and 15 of *Spirit of the Web: The Age of Information from Telegraph to Internet*. Toronto: Thomas Allen, 2006.

8   By March 1923 the US had issued 556 broadcasting licences; Canada had thirty-four licensed operators.

9   As of 2013, nearly 650 CRTC-authorized television services and more than a thousand radio services were available in Canada.

10 About fifteen percent of Canadian homes had radio receivers at that time; the number would double over the next two years.

11 F.W. Peers, *The Politics of Canadian Broadcasting, 1920 to 1951*. Toronto: University of Toronto Press, 1973, p. 20.

12 Assisting the seventy-three-year old Aird were Augustin Frigon, an electrical engineer and director of the École polytechnique in Montreal, and Charles Bowman, editor of the *Ottawa Citizen*.

13 Peers, *op. cit.*, p. 47 – 48.

14 The delay in implementing the Commission's recommendations was also due to a court challenge to the federal government's claim of jurisdiction over broadcasting. It came from Quebec and New Brunswick, and was settled in Ottawa's favour in 1932.

15 Regulatory restrictions on advertising would, in later years, when corporations had firmly established their "personhood," be framed as a free-speech issue. Less frequently heard is the argument that advertising on publicly financed radio and television amounts to a public subsidy to private business, since advertising revenue covers only a small portion of capital and operating costs involved in running a public-service network.

16 Spry and Plaunt were thirty and twenty-six, respectively.

17 Quoted in Peers, *op. cit.*, p. 40.

18 *Ibid.*, p. 55.

19 The lack of coverage of the rest of Canada on SRC is striking. See the intervention of Senator Pierre de Bané, "The Trouble With Radio-Canada," CTRC, Nov. 17, 2012, CBC/SRC licence renewal hearings: https://services.crtc.gc.ca/pub/ListeInterventionList/Documents.aspx?ID=174810&Lang=e.

CHAPTER 2

20 Roger Bird, ed., *Documents of Canadian Broadcasting*. Ottawa: Carlton University Press, 1968. p. 254.

21 Canadian's public broadcaster was initially financed through an annual license fee for radio receivers that grew to $2.50 by 1953. When television arrived, the anticipated costs were enormous; it was estimated a license fee of $15 per set was needed to cover them. This was deemed to be politically impossible: Canadians, many of whom were able to receive "free" television signals from American border stations, found it difficult to understand why they should be asked to pay a license fee for Canadian programming. Instead, the radio license was dropped, and a fifteen percent excise tax was imposed on radio and television sets and parts. This brought in more than enough money for the CBC's operations in the first couple of years, but as the market for TV sets became saturated, revenue quickly fell below what was needed even to maintain existing services. (The BBC continues to be financed through a license fee arrangement.)

22 The six were Halifax, Montreal, Toronto, Winnipeg, Edmonton, and Vancouver.

23 Knowlton Nash, *The Swashbucklers: the Story of Canada's Battling*

Broadcasters. Toronto: McClelland and Stewart, 2001. p. 185.

24   *Ibid.*, p. 180, Spry was writing in *Queen's Quarterly* journal.

25   CRTC, Chart 4.0.5 "Communications Monitoring Report 2014: Broadcasting System."

26   Massey Report, www.collectionscanada.gc.ca/massey/h5-400-e.html.

27   Applebaum-Hébert also recommended shutting down the National film Board of Canada and turning it into a film school.

28   Sid Adelman, "Applebert wants NBC North; NBC wishes it was CBC South" *Toronto Star* Nov. 28, 1982: D2.

29   A problem associated with leveraged takeovers has been that the enormous debt loads they generate for the purchaser almost inevitably leads to massive layoffs and related service cuts, to reduce costs in the target firm.

30   Standing Committee on Canadian Heritage, *Lincoln Committee Report,* 2003, p. 596. The report commented: "Given that all of these proposed services suit the mandate of a public broadcaster, the Committee cannot understand why the Corporation was denied these services by the CRTC."

31   David Demers and Donna Merskin, "Corporate news structure and the managerial revolution," *Journal of Media Economics* 13.2 (2000): 103 – 121.

32   Dwayne Winseck, "Financialization and the 'Crisis of the Media:' The Rise and Fall of (Some) Media Conglomerates in Canada," *Canadian Journal of Communication* 35 (2010): 365 – 393.

CHAPTER 3

33   Nash, *op. cit.,* p. 183.

34   *Ibid.*, p. 182.

35 Bird, *op. cit.,* p. 338 – 339.

36 Armstrong Consulting for CBC: "The 2014 Media Environ-
    ment: Information for the Board of Directors" Nov. 19, 2014,
    p. 13.

37 Robert Armstrong, *Broadcasting Policy in Canada.* Toronto: Uni-
    versity of Toronto Press, 2010, p. 107.

38 http://laws-lois.justice.gc.ca/eng/acts/B-9.01.

39 Section 3.1 (l) and (m). See Appendix 1.

40 Section 3.1 (e) and (f). See Appendix 1.

41 The CRTC imposed thirty percent Canadian content mini-
    mums on AM radio in 1972 in the face of heavy opposition
    from the private radio industry. Forecasts of financial disaster
    proved to be hyperbolic and illusory.

42 For a concise digest, see Robert Armstrong, *Broadcasting Policy in
    Canada.* Toronto: University of Toronto Press, 2010, Chapter
    6. See also www.crtc.gc.ca/eng/cancon.htm.

CHAPTER 4

43 Michael Tracey, *The Decline and Fall of Public Service Broadcasting.*
    New York: Oxford University Press, 1990, p. 25.

44 Remaining provincial public broadcasters are TV Ontario
    and its French-language equivalent TFO, British Columbia's
    Knowledge, and Télé-Québec, which is government-owned
    but advertising-supported. Saskatchewan's SCN network, a
    strong regional presence on television, was privatized in 2010
    by the government of Premier Brad Wall and eventually sold to
    Rogers Media. "SCN's viewership is quite low," Dustin Dun-
    can, the Minister of Tourism, Parks, Culture and Sport, said at
    the time. "We feel that there is no longer a role for government

in the broadcast business." Alberta sold its Access educational channel in 1995: it eventually ended up in the hands of Bell Media, and now exists as CTV Two, a commercial specialty channel that carries some educational content alongside conventional network TV fare.

45   The UNESCO publication "Public Broadcasting: Why? How?" defines public broadcasting as follows: "Neither commercial nor State-controlled, public broadcasting's only raison d'être is public service. It is the public's broadcasting organization; it speaks to everyone as a citizen. Public broadcasters encourage access to and participation in public life. They develop knowledge, broaden horizons, and enable people to better understand themselves by better understanding the world and others. Public broadcasting is defined as a meeting place where all citizens are welcome and considered equals. It is an information and education tool, accessible to all and meant for all, whatever their social or economic status. Its mandate is not restricted to information and cultural development—public broadcasting must also appeal to the imagination, and entertain. But it does so with a concern for quality that distinguishes it from commercial broadcasting. Because it is not subject to the dictates of profitability, public broadcasting must be daring and innovative, and take risks. And when it succeeds in developing outstanding genres or ideas, it can impose its high standards and set the tone for other broadcasters. For some, such as British author Anthony Smith, writing about the British Broadcasting Corporation—seen by many as the cradle of public broadcasting—it is so important that it has 'probably been the greatest of the instruments of social democracy of the century'." www.

unesco.org.

46   The Canadian Association of Broadcasters (CAB), the private
broadcasting industry's chief lobbyist, was founded in 1926. A
record of its opposition to the CBC can be found in E. Austin
Weir, *The Struggle for National Broadcasting in Canada*. Minneapolis: University of Minnesota Press, 1965.

47   Canadian Media Research Inc., "CBC in Crisis: New Strategic
Directions." mediatrends-research.blogspot.com.

48   Graham Murdoch, "Public Broadcasting and Democratic Culture," in Janet Wasco, ed., *A Companion to Television*. New York:
Wiley, 2009, p. 192.

49   Canadian Media Research Inc. media trends survey.

50   John Reith, *op. cit.*

51   An interesting contrast to Reithian principles is found in the
founding mission statement of the American public radio system, NPR. Written in 1970 by founder and first program director Bill Siemering, it reflects a typically American emphasis on the individual as opposed to the collectivity: "National
Public Radio will serve the individual: it will promote personal growth; it will regard the individual differences among
men with respect and joy rather than derision and hate; it will
celebrate the human experience as infinitely varied rather than
vacuous and banal; it will encourage a sense of active constructive participation, rather than apathetic helplessness." The complete statement can be found at http://current.org/2012/05/
national-public-radio-purposes.

52   Quoted in Tracey, *op. cit*, p. 67.

53   *Ibid.*, p. 67.

54   *Ibid.*, p. 82.

55   *Ibid.*, p. 85.

56   *Ibid.*, p. 88.

57   Produced or the BBC by UK-based Inflection Point research
     group. www.bbc.co.uk/aboutthebbc/insidethebbc/howwe-
     work/reports/bbc_report_public_and_private_broadcasting.
     html.

CHAPTER 5

58   Richard Stursberg, *Tower of Babble: Sins, Secrets and Successes In-
     side the CBC.* Toronto: Douglas and McIntyre, 2012.

59   *Ibid.*, p. 80.

60   *Ibid.*, p. 81.

61   *Ibid.*, p. 18.

62   One need not look to other countries for evidence of what is
     possible on television: the CBC's own schedule for 1960 – 1961
     provides an insight into what used to be considered normal fare
     on the network. *Festival* in that year presented Shakespeare's
     Julius Caesar, an adaptation of Dickens' *Great Expectations*; a
     Stratford Festival performance of *H.M.S. Pinafore*; the operas
     Electra and *Falstaff*; Eugene O'Neil's *The Great God Brown*; Jean
     Anouilh's *Ring Around the Moon* and *Colombe*; S. Ansky's *The
     Dibbuk*; Oscar Wilde's *Lord Arthur Saville's Crime*; James Re-
     aney's *The Killdeer*; Emlyn Williams' *Night Must Fall*; Henry
     James' *The Pupil.* The new program *Q for Quest* hosted by An-
     drew Allen presented in the same season interviews with Mor-
     decai Richler, Maureen Forrester, James Reaney and others,
     and performances of Len Peterson's *Burlap Bags*; Brecht's *The
     Great Scholar Wu*; Chekov's *For the Information of Husbands*; The-
     odore Bikel and Mary Martin in *The Sound of Music*; *The World of*

S.J. Perelman; a performance by Lambert, Hendricks, and Ross; Jean Cocteau's *The Human Voice* and much more. In the season of 1956 – 1957 "L'Heure du concert" presented fourteen operas including Stravinsky's *Oedipus Rex* and Gounod's *Mireille*, plus six ballets, including the National Ballet's *Swan Lake*. Also in that year, the English television network broadcast forty-eight dramas a week, more than half of them written by Canadians. *Folio* scheduled twelve plays, half by Canadian writers; *General Motors Theatre* presented eighteen hour-long plays including Arthur Hailey's *Flight Into Danger*; *On Camera* presented another twenty-nine half-hour plays, most of them Canadian. (Weir 393ff.)

63 Rabinovitch said of his own tenure as CBC president: "I approached the job as a businessman. I looked at how our assets could generate money. I sold Newsworld International, I leveraged our real estate holdings. The bottom line is that I did not suffer from losses. I created more cash flow, which allowed us to enhance the quality of our programs, take more risks, try more series, update the delivery system to a digital model—and in the long run, save more money." Interview with Greg O'Brien: www.cartt.ca/article/i-really-doubt-cbc-going-be-able-compete-future-says-former-ceo.

64 Stursberg, *op. cit.*, p. 247.

65 Stursberg, *op. cit.*, p. 247 – 248.

66 The CBC under current management apparently does not consider product placement to be advertising. CBC Policy 1.3.8 states: "The CBC/Radio-Canada does not accept advertising of any kind in programming and Websites designated by the CBC/Radio-Canada as directed to children under twelve years of age. Products that appeal to children and in their normal use require

adult supervision may not be advertised in station breaks adjacent to children's programs."

67   In 2015, the BBC Trust approved product placement in sponsored programming on its BBC World News channel, which is distributed internationally as a cable specialty channel. This followed a decision by the Conservative government of the day to stop funding the BBC World Service operations directly as a foreign affairs initiative, transferring that responsibility to the BBC. The BBC earns revenue from a number of commercial channels worldwide, including BBC Canada. This money helps to support the BBC's commercial-free domestic operations.

68   Stursberg, *op. cit.*, p. 262.

69   *Ibid.*, p. 251 – 252.

70   http://mediatrends-research.blogspot.ca/2012/04/cbc-ex-cbc-executives-and-factortion.html.

71   John Doyle, *Globe and Mail,* Sept. 10, 2012.

72   Stursberg, *op. cit.,* p. 23.

73   Stursberg, *op. cit.*, p 24.

74   Todd Gitlin, *Inside Prime Time.* New York: Routledge, 1994, p. 27. He adds: "Network executives often say their problem is simple. Their tradition, in a sense, is the search for steady profits. They want above all to put on the air shows best calculated to accumulate maximum reliable audiences. Maximum audiences attract maximum dollars for advertisers, and advertiser dollars are, after all, the network's objective. (Network executives recite the point so predictably, so confidently, they sound like vulgar Marxists.)." *Ibid.*, p. 21.

75   Gresham's Law was formulated in the sixteenth century by Sir John Gresham, who noticed that when coins containing different

amounts of precious metal have the same face value as currency, shopkeepers and others will tend to hoard the more valuable coinage while using the less valuable for payment and making change. Thus, the "bad" coinage drives the "good" out of circulation.

76 The all-time top thirty (of fifty, compiled January 2010): *The Sopranos* (HBO); *Brideshead Revisited* (ITV, 1981); *Our Friends in the North* (BBC, 1996); *Mad Men* (AMC, 2007 –); *A Very peculiar Practice* (BBC, 1986 – 1988); *Talking Heads* (BBC, 1988, 1998); *The Singing Detective* (BBC, 1986); *Oranges Are Not The Only Fruit* (BBC, 1990); *State of Play* (BBC, 2003); *Boys from the Blackstuff* (BBC, 1982); *The West Wing* (NBC, 1999 – 2006); *Twin Peaks* (ABC, 1990 – 1991); *Queer as Folk* (Channel 4, 1999 – 2000); *The Wire* (HBO, 2002 – 2008); *Six Feet Under* (HBO, 2001 – 2005); *How Do You Want Me* (BBC, 1998 – 1999); *Smiley's People* (BBC, 1982); *House of Cards* (BBC, 1990); *Prime Suspect* (ITV, 1991 – 2006); *Bodies* (BBC, 2004 – 2006); *Tinker, Tailor, Soldier, Spy* (BBC, 1979); *Buffy the Vampire Slayer* (The WB/UPN, 1997 – 2003); *Cracker* (ITV, 1993 – 1996); *Pennies from Heaven* (BBC, 1978); *Battlestar Galactica* (Sci-Fi/Sky 2003 – 2009); *Coronation Street* (ITV, 1960 –); *The Jewel in the Crown* (ITV, 1984); *The Monocled Mutineer* (BBC, 1986); *Clocking Off* (BBC, 2000 – 2003); *Inspector Morse* (ITV, 1987 – 2000). In the international reader comments that followed the posting, the program most referenced as should-have-been-there was another BBC production, *I, Claudius* (BBC, 1976).

77 E. Austin Weir, *The Struggle for National Broadcasting in Canada*. Minneapolis: University of Minnesota Press, 1965, p. 313.

78 NPR (formerly National Public Radio) in the US provides an apt illustration. NPR receives half of its funding from lo-

cal member stations, which in turn raise money through pledge drives, corporate underwriting, state and local governments, universities, and the federal Corporation for Public Broadcasting. Since most federal funding was cut off in the 1980s, the occasional over-the-air corporate underwriting spots, which by law can include descriptions of services and contact information, but not specific pitches for products or services, have become much more frequent and intrusive. More recently, NPR has aggressively pursued advertising of all kinds on its websites. To call the NPR network and its affiliates non-commercial is today stretching a point, as they subsist by selling audiences to corporate sponsors. Similarly, since 2011 the US Public Broadcasting Service (PBS) has been incorporating institutional advertising breaks on television at fifteen-minute intervals within its most popular programs, as opposed to the former practice of confining these to the beginning and ending of programs.

79   Britain's commercial ITV system, which has produced programming of exceptionally high quality over the years, can be considered a special case due to the onerous public-service stipulations attached by Parliament to its operating charter, and to the unusually high benchmark established by its competition, the BBC. The statutory public-service requirements had the effect of ameliorating the impact of Gresham's Law; the BBC's well-established standards had produced a discriminating audience pool resistant to cheap, shoddy programs.

80   Richard Rudin, *Broadcasting in the 21st Century*. New York: Palgrave Macmillan, 2011, p. 129.

81   Stursberg, *op. cit.*, p. 23.

CHAPTER 6

82   Stursberg, *op. cit.*, p. 11.

83   Irene Costera Meijer, "Impact or Content," *European Journal of Communications* 20 (2005): 27.

CHAPTER 7

84   See Knowlton Nash, *The Microphone Wars: A History of Triumph and Betrayal at the CBC* for an excellent history of the corporation's news division, and much else.

85   Public Notice, CRTC 1999 – 1997, "Building on Success – A Policy Framework for Canadian Television," para. 47. Note, however, the Commission's strong objection to a Bell Media executive's meddling in CTV News production, discussed in the Introduction.

86   Bruce A. Williams and Michael X. Della Carpini, "The Eroding Boundaries between News and Entertainment and What They Mean for Democratic Politics," in Lee Wilkins and Clifford G. Christians, eds., *The Handbook of Mass Media Ethics*. New York: Taylor and Francis, 2009.

87   Frank is quoted in a classic of television scholarship, Edward Jay Epstein, *News from Nowhere: Television and the News,* p. 40.

88   Ninety percent say they find TV news reliable; thirty-three percent say the same of Internet-based sources: http://blogs.vancouversun.com/2011/05/11/ubc-study-finds-canadians-trust-mainstream-news-media-more-than-social-networks. Average weekly viewing hours for TV news: "CRTC Communications Monitoring Report 2014: Broadcasting System."

89   See, for example, Robert W. McChesney, *The Political Economy of Media: Enduring Issues, Emerging Dilemmas*. New York:

Monthly Review Press, 2008, p.124. Over the past twenty years, newsroom staffs have shrunk by thirty to fifty percent across the North American industry.

90   Wade Rowland, *Greed, Inc. Why Corporations Rule our World and How We Let It Happen*. New York: Arcade Publishing, 2012.

91   Ken Auletta. *Three Blind Mice: How the TV Networks Lost Their Way*. New York: Random House, 1991.

92   Pew Research Centre, "State of the News Media 2014." www.journalism.org/2014/03/26/state-of-the-news-media-2014-overview.

93   www.gallup.com/poll/155585/americans-confidence-television-news-drops-new-low.aspx. This is higher than confidence in the written press at forty-four percent.

94   William Horsley, "Public Trust in the Media: Why is it Declining?" Report for the Association of European Journalists.

95   http://blogs.vancouversun.com/2011/05/11/ubc-study-finds-canadians-trust-mainstream-news-media-more-than-social-networks. Confidence in newspapers among Canadians was an identical ninety percent.

96   Anglophone Canadians eighteen and over. "Who is Canada's News Leader?" *Canadian Media Research Inc.*, March 2012. http://mediatrends-research.blogspot.ca/2012/03/who-is-canadas-tv-news-leader-who-is.html.

97   For a report on Williams's travails, providing insight into the world of commercial news, see www.vanityfair.com/news/2015/04/nbc-news-brian-williams-scandal-comcast.

98   www.thestar.com/news/gta/2015/01/22/cbc-will-no-longer-approve-paid-appearances-by-on-air-journalists-memo-states.html

99   http://fusion.net/story/148718/journalism-art-ethics.

100 www.theguardian.com/commentisfree/2013/mar/27/no-
     golden-age-journalism-news-media-end-times.

101 www.winnipegfreepress.com/opinion/blogs/cox/264944996.
     html.

102 www.Alexa.com., March 2015 rankings.

103 www.cjr.org/realtalk/this_is_the_best_moment_to_be.php.

CHAPTER 8

104 On an international scale, a comparison of nineteen countries
     according to their preference for domestic programs places Ja-
     pan and the US first (all of the top one hundred programs are
     domestic) with the UK and most of Europe weighing in at
     around ninety of the top one hundred. Even at the bottom of
     the scale, Ireland and Australia can claim local origination for
     sixty-one and fifty-nine of their respective top one hundreds.
     English Canada places last, with just twenty-three of the top
     one hundred programs being of domestic origin. French Can-
     ada's domestic programming comes in at a respectable seventy-
     five of the top one hundred.

105 Mark J. Kasoff, Patrick James, *Canadian Studies in the New Mil-
     lennium*. Toronto: University of Toronto Press, 2013, p. 420.

106 "Mémoires Vives," 35, Dec. 2012. Outside Quebec, in the
     French-speaking minority communities of Atlantic Canada,
     Ontario, and across the West, demands for a separate French-
     language network arose almost immediately, and were not sat-
     isfied by the bilingual programming on the early CRBC and
     CBC networks. So-called French programming was mostly
     instrumental music, and in a notorious example of corporate

insensitivity, the CRBC's western stations failed, in 1934, to broadcast celebrations in Gaspé marking the 400th anniversary of Jacques Cartier's arrival in Canada. Throughout the 1930s and 1940s a concerted campaign to build a handful of French-language, private, CBC affiliates met with only limited success; subscription campaigns raised required funding, but the CBC, as regulator, was slow to grant licences in Saskatchewan and Alberta. CKSB St. Boniface/Winnipeg, the first of these stations, was licensed in 1946, but it was not until 1952 that the CBC formally organized a Western French-language network supplying affiliate stations across the prairie provinces with sixteen hours of programming a day and covering the cost of transmission lines from Montreal. The network was effectively incorporated as Radio-Canada in 1973.

107 Stursberg, *op. cit.*, p. 122.
108 *The Growth of the Network Media Economy in Canada*, 1984 – 2013, Canadian Media Concentration Research Project, No. 4, 2013. www.cmcrp.org.
109 Jean-Pierre Blais, Speech to Canadian Club, March 12, 2015.
110 Irene Costa Meijer, "Impact or Content," *European Journal of Communications* 20 (2005): 27 – 53; BBC/Inflection Point, *op. cit.*
111 Philip Savage, "Identity Housekeeping in Canadian Public Service Media," in Petros Iosifidis, ed., *Reinventing Public Service Communication*. London: Palgrave Macmillan, 2010, p. 281 – 284.
112 Among anglophones eighteen and over. Canadian Media Research Inc., 2012.
113 Canadian Media Research Inc., "CBC in Crisis: New Strategic Directions." April 2, 2014, p. 16.
114 Stursberg, *op, cit.*, p. 233.

115 www.statcan.gc.ca/daily-quotidien/100526/dq100526b-eng.
htm.

116 Stursberg, *op, cit.*, p. 236.

117 *Globe and Mail*, May 29, 2008.

118 Stursberg, *op. cit.*, p. 238 – 239.

119 Audience share for CBC Radio One: 8.7% in 2000; 12.5% in 2013. For Radio 2: 3.6% in 2000; 3.1% in 2013. Audience share for Ici Radio-Canada Première (formerly Première Chaîne [Radio One]) in 2000: 6.9%; in 2013 16.8%. For Ici Musique (formerly Espace Musique) (Radio 2): 2.0% in 2000; 4.6% in 2013. CBC Research and Analysis, "2014 Media Environment, Information for the Board of Directors," Nov. 19, 2014.

120 Weir, *op. cit.*, p. 273.

121 Most of this scheduling information has been gleaned from Austin Weir's invaluable and exhaustive first-person account of early public-service broadcasting in Canada.

122 Canadian Media Research Inc., "CBC in Crisis: New Strategic Directions," April 2, 2014.

CHAPTER 9

123 Canadians, on average, spend forty-five hours a month on the Internet, evenly splitting their time between accessing audio and video, and other activities such as keeping in touch on social media, doing research, or dealing with email.

124 CBC, "2014 Media Environment," *op. cit.*, p. 82.

125 Richard Nielsen, "Broadcasting Policy Position Paper," unpublished, 2012.

126 *Ibid.*

127 In this connection, see the BBC documentary "All Watched

Over By Machines of Loving Grace," 2013.

128 In October 2012, however, the federal government was able to allocate $25 million to the Museum of Civilization to change its name to the Canadian Museum of History and develop an annex displaying Canadian historical artifacts.

129 For an eye-opening look at the blogosphere, see Ryan Holiday, *Trust Me, I'm Lying: the tactics and confessions of a media manipulator.* Toronto: Penguin Group, 2012.

130 Kirstine Stewart, Executive Vice-President, CBC English Services, speech to Canadian Telecom Summit, June 6, 2012.

131 Prior to the recent introduction of "portable people meters" in the ratings industry, the average number of viewing hours had been estimated at about twenty-seven hours. The discrepancy results from the fact that people meters measure more than whether a television set is turned on—they measure how many people are watching (or are at least in the room).

132 "No, Canadians Are NOT Watching Less TV," *Canadian Media Research Inc.*, March 2012. http://mediatrends-research.blogspot.ca/2012/03/no-canadians-are-not-watching-less-tv.html.

133 *Ibid.*

134 However, in 2012, as part of the government-mandated conversion to digital television in Canada, the CBC shut down more than 650 low-power re-transmitters all over the country, arguing that and most of the re-transmitters were no longer necessary to its universal coverage mandate since remaining high-powered digital transmitters covered ninety-seven percent of the population, and ninety percent now had cable or satellite access. More than one hundred TVO, TFO and Télé-Québec re-transmitters

were closed at the same time. Re-transmitters are a rarity in the private broadcasting industry, which converted to digital TV in 2012 as well. In 2014 a request from BDUs to shut down some private TV transmitters and deliver content directly to cable as a cost-saving measure was denied by the CRTC, which continues to require that conventional television stations have at least one transmitter in order to qualify for the $250 million subsidy program known as simultaneous substitution (sim-sub).

CHAPTER 10

135 Government of Canada. *Broadcasting Act*, 1991, Section 3 (see Appendix 1).

136 CRTC, 2014. Concentration of ownership in Canadian commercial media is remarkable: Bell Canada (BCE) purchased CTV, the nation's largest commercial television network, for $1.3 billion in 2010, and formed Bell Media. Bell Media owns twenty-eight television stations and thirty specialty cable channels, including TSN. In 2011 Bell teamed with Rogers Communications to purchase Maple Leafs Sports and Entertainment, owners of Toronto Maple Leafs and other sports properties, for $1.6 billion. Bell also owns a minority stake in the Montreal Canadiens. In 2012 Bell Media (annual revenue c. $20 billion) purchased Astral Media, operator of twenty-five television specialty channels including HBO Canada, and eight-four radio stations, for $3.4 billion. Bell's share of the Canadian television audience in 2014 was about forty percent. Rogers Communications Inc. (annual revenue c. $5 billion), Canada's biggest cable provider, owns five CityTV television stations in the country's major cities, a clutch of specialty cable channels including

Sportsnet, and fifty-one radio stations. In 2014, it outbid the CBC for rights to NHL hockey, the country's biggest sports media franchise. Shaw Media (annual revenue c. $2.5 billion), also a major cable provider, owns Global Television Network and eighteen cable specialty channels. Quebecor (annual revenue c. $4.3 billion), Quebec's dominant cable provider, in 2000 bought the French-language commercial network TVA and established Quebecor Media, which launched the unsuccessful cable channel Sun News. Telus (annual revenue c. $12 billion) is Canada's second-largest telecom company, providing cable services in Alberta and British Columbia, plus Internet and telephone services. Together these enormously profitable giants claim eight-six percent of total BDU revenue, and a substantial majority of the Canadian radio and television audience.

137 Weir, *op cit.*, p. 262.

138 Bruce Steele, private correspondence, 2015.

139 Armstrong Consulting, in CBC, "2014 Media Environment," *op. cit.*, p. 13. Because it airs primarily Canadian programs, CBC Television does not benefit to any significant degree from either advertising replacement, simultaneous substitution, or section 19.1 subsidies (and CBC Radio not at all).

140 Nordicity, CRTC, in CBC, "2014 Media Environment," *ibid.*, p. 2.

141 Barry Kiefl, "Domino effect snowballing into a chain reaction." Canadian Media Research Inc. blog post, Sept. 5, 2012.

142 Canadian Media Research Inc. blog, April 28, 2014.

143 Pilkington Report: "Report on the Committee on Broadcasting." London: HMSO,1962, p.147, para. 504.

144 http://fair.org/blog/2013/05/21/problems-at-pbs-from-rose-

to-koch.

145   CRTC, summarized in CBC, "2014 Media Environment: Information for the Board of Directors," Nov, 19, 2014.

146   The BBC, like all European Union public broadcasters, has in recent years been required to justify its expenditures on sports programming within the context of the wider broadcasting market under EU guidelines. That is, they must demonstrate that in bidding for broadcast rights, they are not unfairly competing with their commercial counterparts by, for example, bidding up prices or monopolizing key rights.

147   Mary Jane Miller, *Rewind and Search: Conversations with the Makers and Decision-Makers of CBC Television Drama*. Kingston: McGill-Queen's University Press, 1996. p. xiv. On this subject, see also E. Austin Weir, *The Struggle for National Broadcasting in Canada*. Minneapolis: University of Minnesota Press, 1965.

148   Tracey, *op. cit.*, p. 266.

149   Nielsen, *op. cit.* Tony Manera, who was appointed from inside the CBC, is an exception.

150   The media watchdog Friends of Canadian Broadcasting reports that since 1936, eighty-seven percent of appointees have been affiliated with the governing party.

APPENDIX

Section 3 of the Broadcasting Act, 1991

3. (1) It is hereby declared as the broadcasting policy for Canada that

(*a*) the Canadian broadcasting system shall be effectively owned and controlled by Canadians;

(*b*) the Canadian broadcasting system, operating primarily in the English and French languages and comprising public, private and community elements, makes use of radio frequencies that are public property and provides, through its programming, a public service essential to the maintenance and enhancement of national identity and cultural sovereignty;

(*c*) English and French language broadcasting, while sharing common aspects, operate under different conditions and may have different requirements;

(*d*) the Canadian broadcasting system should

(i) serve to safeguard, enrich and strengthen the cultural, political, social and economic fabric of Canada,

(ii) encourage the development of Canadian expression by providing a wide range of programming that reflects Canadian attitudes, opinions, ideas, values and artistic creativity, by displaying Canadian talent in entertainment programming and by offering information and analysis concerning Canada and other countries from a Canadian point of view,

(iii) through its programming and the employment opportunities arising out of its operations, serve the needs and interests, and reflect the circumstances and aspirations, of Canadian men, women and children, including equal rights, the linguistic duality and multicultural and multiracial nature of Canadian society and the special place of aboriginal peoples within that society, and

(iv) be readily adaptable to scientific and technological change;

(e) each element of the Canadian broadcasting system shall contribute in an appropriate manner to the creation and presentation of Canadian programming;

(f) each broadcasting undertaking shall make maximum use, and in no case less than predominant use, of Canadian creative and other resources in the creation and presentation of programming, unless the nature of the service provided by the undertaking, such as specialized content or format or the use of languages other than French and English, renders that use impracticable, in which case the undertaking shall make the greatest practicable use of those resources;

g) the programming originated by broadcasting undertakings should be of high standard;

(h) all persons who are licensed to carry on broadcasting undertakings have a responsibility for the programs they broadcast;

(i) the programming provided by the Canadian broadcasting system should

(i) be varied and comprehensive, providing a balance of information, enlightenment and entertainment for men, women and children of all ages, interests and tastes,

(ii) be drawn from local, regional, national and international sources,

(iii) include educational and community programs,

(iv) provide a reasonable opportunity for the public to be exposed to the expression of differing views on matters of public concern, and

(v) include a significant contribution from the Canadian independent production sector;

(j) educational programming, particularly where provided through the facilities of an independent educational authority, is an integral part of the Canadian broadcasting system;

(k) a range of broadcasting services in English and in French shall be extended to all Canadians as resources become available;

(l) the Canadian Broadcasting Corporation, as the national public broadcaster, should provide radio and television services incorporating a wide range of programming that informs, enlightens and entertains;

(m) the programming provided by the Corporation should

(i) be predominantly and distinctively Canadian,

(ii) reflect Canada and its regions to national and regional audiences, while serving the special needs of those regions,

(iii) actively contribute to the flow and exchange of cultural expression,

(iv) be in English and in French, reflecting the different needs and circumstances of each official language community, including the particular needs and circumstances of English and French linguistic minorities,

(v) strive to be of equivalent quality in English and in French,

(vi) contribute to shared national consciousness and identity,

(vii) be made available throughout Canada by the most appropriate and efficient means and as resources become available for the purpose, and

(viii) reflect the multicultural and multiracial nature of Canada;

(*n*) where any conflict arises between the objectives of the Corporation set out in paragraphs (*l*) and (*m*) and the interests of any other broadcasting undertaking of the Canadian broadcasting system, it shall be resolved in the public interest, and where the public interest would be equally served by resolving the conflict in favour of either, it shall be resolved in favour of the objectives set out in paragraphs (*l*) and (*m*);

(*o*) programming that reflects the aboriginal cultures of Canada should be provided within the Canadian broadcasting system as resources become available for the purpose;

(*p*) programming accessible by disabled persons should be provided within the Canadian broadcasting system as resources become available for the purpose;

(*q*) without limiting any obligation of a broadcasting undertaking to provide the programming contemplated by paragraph (*i*), alternative television programming services in English and in French should be provided where necessary to ensure that the full range of programming contemplated by that paragraph is made available through the Canadian broadcasting system;

(r) the programming provided by alternative television programming services should

(i) be innovative and be complementary to the programming provided for mass audiences,

(ii) cater to tastes and interests not adequately provided for by the programming provided for mass audiences, and include programming devoted to culture and the arts,

(iii) reflect Canada's regions and multicultural nature,

(iv) as far as possible, be acquired rather than produced by those services, and

(v) be made available throughout Canada by the most cost-efficient means;

(s) private networks and programming undertakings should, to an extent consistent with the financial and other resources available to them,

(i) contribute significantly to the creation and presentation of Canadian programming, and

(ii) be responsive to the evolving demands of the public; and

(t) distribution undertakings

(i) should give priority to the carriage of Canadian programming services and, in particular, to the carriage of local Canadian stations,

(ii) should provide efficient delivery of programming at affordable rates, using the most effective technologies available at reasonable cost,

(iii) should, where programming services are supplied to them by broadcasting undertakings pursuant to contractual arrangements, provide reasonable terms for the carriage, packaging and retailing of those programming services, and

(iv) may, where the Commission considers it appropriate, originate programming, including local programming, on such terms as are conducive to the achievement of the objectives of the broadcasting policy set out in this subsection, and in particular provide access for underserved linguistic and cultural minority communities.

Marginal note: Further declaration

(2) It is further declared that the Canadian broadcasting system constitutes a single system and that the objectives of the broadcasting policy set out in subsection (1) can best be achieved by providing for the regulation and supervision of the Canadian broadcasting system by a single independent public authority.

ACKNOWLEDGEMENTS

I am indebted to Jeffrey Dvorkin, Paul Gaffney, Barry Kiefl, Eric Koch, Bernie Lucht, Ian Morrison, Alain Pineau, Kealy Wilkinson, Bruce Steele, and Tom Wilson, all of whom have provided valuable ideas and insights. And once again I owe a debt to my publisher Linda Leith for her support and enthusiasm in publishing this book and an earlier essay, *Saving the CBC: Balancing Profit and Public Service* (2013).

INDEX

235